A Book for Grandmothers

ALSO BY RUTH GOODE

People of the Ice Age

The Magic of Walking, with Aaron Sussman

Man and His Body, with Benjamin F. Miller, M.D.

My Love Affair with the State of Maine, with Gertrude MacKenzie

Impresario, A Memoir, with S. Hurok

A Book for Grandmothers

RUTH GOODE

McGraw-Hill Book Company

New York St. Louis San Francisco Bogotá Düsseldorf
Madrid Mexico Montreal Panama Paris
São Paulo Tokyo Toronto

Reprinted by arrangement with
Macmillan Publishing Co., Inc.

First McGraw-Hill Paperback edition, 1977

3456789O FGRFGR 7832109

Library of Congress Cataloging in Publication Data

Goode, Ruth.
A book for grandmothers.

Includes index.
1. Grandmothers. 2. Family—United States.
I. Title.
[HQ759.9.G66 1976b] 301.42'7 77-24727
ISBN 0-07-023740-9

For Gerry
grandfather without peer

Contents

Contents

Foreword: The Grandmother Experience

For me and for every woman I know, no matter how many of our friends have arrived there before us, no matter what we have expected or been told to expect, becoming a grandmother has been a totally new and wonderful but also somewhat strange experience for which nothing seems to have prepared us in advance. And as the children grow and change, we are constantly discovering new aspects of our role in their lives and their effect on ours, even—to our surprise—new aspects of ourselves.

Grandfathers have asked me, and so have fathers looking forward to grandfatherhood, Why a book for grandmothers? What about us?

Despite the title of this book, grandfather will find himself in its pages. We ignore grandfathers at our peril—one of them is looking over my shoulder as I write. They strengthen and sustain us, they keep us from committing grandmotherly follies, and they make their own contribution to the grandchildren's lives. But everyone seems to agree with me that grandfathers need no book to reassure, encourage, or advise them. Grandfathers are made in heaven, born fully formed with the birth of their first grandchild. They are the perfect babysitters, storytellers, playmates, and putters-to-bed. Their role is pure delight.

Grandmother's role is traditionally more complex, and today it is more so than ever. Grandmother flies across continents and oceans in time of trouble, tends sickness, holds everybody's hand through dissension and divorce. She walks a tightrope among grandchildren and step-grandchildren, in-laws and ex-in-laws and step-in-laws, the children's other grandparents and step-grandparents. With daughters and daughters-in-law launching themselves on jobs, professions, and careers, some grandmothers nowadays find themselves back in the mother role, rearing their grandchildren.

For a while there, during the youth revolution of a decade ago, we grandparents were relegated with our grandchildren's parents and everyone else over thirty to a limbo of being unseen and unheard.

But no longer. We are in the midst of a grandmotherly renaissance. We are being rehabilitated, restored, not so much to rights and privileges which may indeed be gone forever, but to responsibilities. Whether we are asked or we volunteer, once more we have a place.

It is not always a comfortable place. As I went about the country, talking to grandparents, parents, young and grown grandchildren, I was astonished at the way the very mention of a book for grandmothers affected people. It opened windows into the whole buzzing hive of changing family life and family relations, and some of this is reflected in the pages that follow.

Good grandmothering can be lighthearted and light-handed. No grandmother needs to become more deeply involved in her children's or grandchildren's lives than she chooses. In some parts of late-twentieth-century America it is still possible to be a traditional grandmother. But the kaleidoscopic patterns are swirling all around us, and as grandmothers we may go swirling dizzily along unless we can find a firm place to put our feet.

To hold up a candle here and there, to light the way along new and sometimes confusing pathways, is what this book is meant to do. As women, wives, mothers, and mothers-in-law, we have managed somehow to make it to this point, and from here on we would like to be—or at least to feel—wiser and surer of ourselves in this challenging, tender, and rewarding new role in the second half of our lives.

Acknowledgments

My indebtedness for help with this book stretches literally from coast to coast and border to border. I owe thanks to grandmothers, daughters, granddaughters, their husbands, sons, brothers, and a bouquet of thanks to my fellow alumnae who joyfully turned a class reunion into a grandmothers' seminar. I have had the privilege of many hours of wise, witty, and illuminating exchanges that made my task a loving labor.

Those whom I have space to thank individually were generous not only with talk but with thoughtful reading and suggestions for the manuscript as it took shape. Martha Winston, of Curtis Brown Ltd., had the idea for such a book and so became in effect the grandmother of this one. Josette Frank, Elsie Lincoln Rosner, Araceli Loomie, Edith Aaron, and Flora Gordon gave unstintingly of their rich experience of grandmothering and of living. My young colleague, Marion Burdick, put her high professional skill into the social and literary research and shared with me her own observations of American family life. I thank these good friends and I hope they will find some virtue in the book to which they contributed so much; for its defects the responsibility is my own.

My gratitude is due also to the authors who have written,

some of them inspiringly, about grandmothers generally, their own grandmothers, and grandmotherhood. Except for the first, the titles of the excerpts were devised for these pages.

Patsy Gray's essay, "What a Grandmother Is," was originally published in *PTA Magazine*, the organ of the National Congress of Parents and Teachers.

"I Am Not Old," is from *My Life History* by Grandma Moses, published by Harper and Brothers.

"Grandmother on Horseback" from Kay Boyle's short story, "Episode in the Life of an Ancestor," can be found in the collection, *Thirty Stories by Kay Boyle*, published by Simon and Schuster.

"That Feeling of Safety" is from *The Autobiography of Bertrand Russell*, in the American publication by Atlantic Little Brown.

"The Sabbath Visit" is from *The Great Fair: Scenes from My Childhood* by Sholem Aleichem, published by Noonday Press.

"A Poem," from *Childhood*, volume I of the *Complete Works of Count Leo Tolstoy*, translated and edited by Leo Wiener, was originally printed by J. M. Dent and Sons, Ltd., London, 1904.

"The Center of Our Household" is from *Blackberry Winter: My Earlier Years*, by Margaret Mead, published by William Morrow and Company.

"Storytelling," from *My Childhood*, by Maxim Gorky, can be found in *Autobiography of Maxim Gorky*, translated by Isidor Schneider, in the American edition published by Citadel Press.

"My Grandmother's Domain" is from *Of a World That Is No More* by Isaac Bashevis Singer, published by Vanguard Press.

"In the Rain" is from *Swann's Way* by Marcel Proust, in

the translation by C. K. Scott Moncrieff in The Modern Library.

"The Magic Lantern" is from *The Grandmothers, a Family Portrait* by Glenway Westcott, published by Harper and Brothers.

"Differentness Begins At Home" is from *Grandma Called It Carnal*, published by Michael Joseph Ltd., London.

"A Refuge" is from *My Nights and Days* by "Julie," published by G. P. Putnam's Sons.

"Elder Victorians" is from *The Scarlet Tree* by Osbert Sitwell, published by The Macmillan Company, London.

"This Astonishing Old Age," including George Sand's letter on her sixty-fourth birthday, is from *Lélia, the Life of George Sand*, by André Maurois, translated by Gerard Hopkins, published by Harper and Brothers.

My acknowledgments to the publishers and translators of these works.

R. G.

A Book for Grandmothers

What a Grandmother Is

A grandmother is a lady who has no children of her own, so she likes other people's little girls. A grandfather is a man grandmother. He goes for walks with boys, and they talk about fishing and tractors and like that.

Grandmas don't have to do anything except be there. They are old, so they shouldn't play hard or run. It is enough if they drive us to the market where the pretend horse is and have lots of dimes ready. Or if they take us for walks, they slow down past things like pretty leaves or caterpillars. They should never "Hurry up."

Usually they are fat, but not too fat to tie the kids' shoes. They wear glasses, and they can take their teeth and gums off. It is better if they don't typewrite or play cards, except with us. They don't have to be smart, only answer questions like why dogs chase cats or how come God isn't married.

They don't talk baby talk like visitors do, because it is hard to understand. When they read to us they don't skip words or mind if it is the same story again.

Everybody should try to have one, especially if you don't have television, because grandmas are the only grown-ups who have got time.

—"What a Grandmother Is," by Patsy Gray, aged 9

I

Something Really New

The arrival of a new baby is surely one of life's most marvelous events. It fills us with awe and wonder, and when we participate in it as grandparents it adds an exhilarating new dimension to our lives.

We hold it in our arms, tantalized by the ineffable mystery of its inheritance, to which we, too, have added our bit. This is no little empty vessel, as we used to be told, no little hollow pitcher into which we will pour the ingredients of a new personality. We know now that it comes to us with its mind already made up, as one might say, its unique genetic endowment already encoded for the kind of person it is capable of becoming.

Looking into the tiny wizened face of the newborn—so transiently prophetic of the future adult—we search for family resemblances, try to guess at family traits and talents hidden there. Whom will this enigmatic little person take after? What novel blend of our pooled characteristics will it reveal?

In all the excitement of its arrival, the hustle and bustle of welcoming it into the world, we can scarcely stop to think what its coming can actually mean to us, its grandparents. Only later, when we have helped to see to its comfort, do we begin to realize what has happened to us. Our first grandchild is the herald of a new phase in our lives, and every grandchild that comes after will reaffirm the wonder of it.

Our grandchildren expand and enhance our lives in ways that reach deep. They reach back into our past and far into our future. They re-create old joys for us, and promise ever new ones as they grow. As for our present, they can enrich the hours and days if we wish, and as much as we wish. As grandparents we have the choice, always, of how much or how little we are involved with them, and even a little involvement—the one or two visits a year if they live far away—can bring very special pleasures.

Each one of our grandchildren is a fresh, unique experience, a new personality, a small but definite individual with whom we can forge a bond. If we are shy with babies, soon enough we find them toddlers, conversationalists on the telephone, crayon artists sending us pictures, school children writing us awkwardly formed words in block letters and original spellings, teen-agers confiding to us their adolescent joys and griefs. We can enter their lives at any stage with which we feel comfortable. And we enter with an ideal introduction, a passport second only to that of their parents. We are their grandparents.

What we can do for them we learn as we go along—from them, from their parents, from our own feelings and insights, from other grandparents. Grandparents are forever exchanging pictures and stories with other grandparents, and we garner wisdom from others' experience—indeed the harvesting of others' experience is the first function of this book.

What they do for us also comes as a discovery. Grandmothers of long standing speak of it as a second chance. They remember the dreadful mistakes they made, or think they made, as parents, and their grandchildren give them the opportunity to recreate themselves in a more satisfying parental image. This time they are able to say and do the right things, as perhaps they did not, the first time around. And not because they are older, more experienced in life, possibly wiser, but because they are grandparents and not parents, because they are that one delicious step removed from the hourly and daily pressures and responsibilities of child-rearing.

But there is much more that our grandchildren do for us. They rekindle for us the spirit of play, the child's sense of adventure and discovery. Grandparents are always being told that they are living history to their grandchildren, that they give the children the reassurance of their roots, the strengthening awareness of continuity. For me and many grandmothers I have talked to, it works the other way as well. They give *us* continuity. They link us to our own motherhood and childhood years, to our parents and grandparents and the stories we remember of times even earlier than those. And they link us to the future as well. They give us a vested interest in the world in which they will live. They make us aware of the world in which we are living today and helping to create for tomorrow.

And all this at our own choice. We choose how far and how deep our grandparenthood will take us. For perhaps the first time in our lives, as grandparents we have the freedom to take as little or as much as we desire out of this new facet of living that our grandchildren bring to us.

All Kinds of Grandmothers

What Is a Grandmother is the name of a little book that came out a few years ago, a collection of children's answers to the question in the title, gathered by Lee Parr McGrath and Joan Scobey with the help of the children's teachers.

They are young grade school children, six, seven, and eight, and their grandmother image is a dream of cupcakes and apple pie, chicken soup, meatballs, ice cream and candy.

Grandmother is someone "to cudel you when you have the mumphs," "to make you fat and then love you," "to spoil you and save you from your parents."

She also goes to football games and cheers when she doesn't know what's happening, gives you Christmas presents your mother doesn't want you to have, has time to play with you no matter how busy she is. She can tell stories and "ferry tails" twenty-four hours a day. She may be a nice old lady who cries when you bring her flowers, or she may be "cool" and go Halloweening with you and your friends, or she may be "groovy" and ride a Honda. She may need you to protect her when your mother scolds her, or she may tell your parents they are raising you wrong.

All kinds of grandmothers, hardly any two alike.

Another set of revelations of how our grandchildren see us comes from granddaughters in their late teens. They like us to be accepting of new ways and ideas, and to spare them any forceful criticisms of the young people's new social customs. They approve of us when we are independent, with lives of our own, and they like us to look well but not to try to look like girls of sixteen, with the makeup and the false eyelashes and the latest mod costume. Said one articulate young critic, "It is more subtle and effective to remain youthful in one's thinking!"

They take pride in our skills, including such traditional ones as cooking, and they like to see us busy and useful at some kind of work whether paid or volunteer or hobby, or any use of our time and talents that satisfies us. They appreciate everything we have done for them, from telling stories and dressing dolls when they were little to sending them boxes of home-baked goodies in college.

Gratifyingly, these granddaughters devoted the largest space in their comments to recalling these affectionate attentions, enumerating them one by one. But they also pointed out that they did not like to be "*smothered*"—their word—with love and gifts.

They gave almost as much space to grandmother's expressions of interest in them. They valued her caring about them and what they were doing. They liked to know she took pleasure in their accomplishments, in their friends, and was sympathetic to their hopes and plans. Obviously they enjoyed talking over all their concerns with grandmother. And indeed they said so. They welcomed understanding discussions with her as between equals, and they liked having the benefit of her counsel—*as long as she left them free to make their own decisions.*

As for grandmother's role in the family, they were equally forthright. They gave her good marks for generosity with her time, her willingness to babysit and do various family services, to cook and bake her "specialties" for the family's enjoyment. They appreciated her efforts to keep the family together and to make a place for herself by contributing to family life.

But they were very severe with a grandmother who tried to run the family, who interfered with parents' authority over the children, or demanded attention, respect, and service simply because of her senior status. These granddaughters had no patience with matriarchs!

And they disapproved of grandmothers who allowed themselves to be imposed upon. They had no patience with martyrs, either!

On balance that's a reassuring survey of how we look to our grandchildren. They do not take our loving attentions for granted, but remember them with gratitude. They do not shut us out of their lives as they grow up, but welcome our interest and seek our advice. And if they warn us against making power plays—whether with too much authority or too much love, which often comes to the same thing—we surely cannot take offense. Because they make it amply clear that they value our independence as much as they do their own. They want us to be ourselves, as they want the freedom to be themselves.

It is striking that the grandmother these girls portray is in many respects a traditional one, and despite changing times it is still a fair likeness of many of us grandmothers today. Mobility and the fragmentation of families may be the growing trend, but not all the grown children move away. Many grandmothers have their married children in their kitchens and the baby and toddler grandchildren in their back yards almost every day. Many grandmothers continue to be the pivot of their families even when the family branches spread far around the country.

I know a grandmother in Kentucky who is the recycling center for her large family's baby and children's clothes, who will say to a visiting daughter or daughter-in-law, "I want that coat your Ginny is wearing—she's getting too big for it and Mary's Caroline in Denver needs it."

I know another grandmother, who moved from a middle western city to Florida when her husband retired, and who is the family's central news bureau. She sends fat letters off regularly from coast to coast, filled with her own news and news she has received in letters from her children, grandchildren, their aunts and uncles, great-aunts, great-uncles, and cousins of all degrees. Her round robin postal service keeps alive a family network, and it keeps her a very real person in the minds of grandchildren who may see her no more than once a year. Thanks to grandmothers like these, families remain whole no matter how scattered, and a vacation trip for any of their members becomes a stepping-stone series of family reunions from town to town across the country.

There are also many of us who do not see our likeness in the traditional portrait, and have no notion of ourselves as the center of an extended kinship network. It may be that our families are small as well as scattered, and there is really not much to be a center of. Then there are those of us who began breaking away from tradition in our girlhood, to follow a job or a profession. Some who are grandmothers today were working women when they married or working mothers afterward, and some of us, as grandmothers, are still working. If we were not traditional mothers, we can scarcely expect to be traditional grandmothers.

But there is a place for every kind of grandmother, traditional and untraditional, and each of us has a choice of the kind she will be.

I Am Not Old

If I didn't start painting, I would have raised chickens. I could still do it now. I would never sit back in a rocking chair, waiting for someone to help me. I have often said, before I would call for help from outsiders, I would rent a room in the city some place and give pancake suppers, just pancake and syrup, and they could have water, like a little breakfast. I never dreamed that the pictures would bring in so much, and as for all that publicity, and as for the fame which came to Grandma so late, that I am too old to care for now. . . .

I felt older when I was 16 than I ever did since. I was old and sedate when I left the Whitesides, I suppose it was the life I led, I had to be so lady-like. Even now I am not old, I never think of it, yet I am a grandmother to 11 grandchildren, I also have 17 great-grandchildren, that's a plenty!

—*My Life History*, by Grandma Moses

2

The First Grandmothers

Grandmothering is an ancient and honorable function, dating back to the first hearth fire in a Stone Age cave. Before men discovered the uses of fire, our ancestors lived like the animals they hunted, following the herds, eating where they killed or found their food, sleeping in any handy shelter. The old folks who could not keep up were simply left behind to live or not. The anthropologists tell us that even up to our own time, some primitive tribes still ritually dispatched the too elderly. (I sometimes wonder how much better we do for them today.)

With the hearth fire, the cave became a home and the horde of hunters and food gatherers became a family. And from then on, grandfathers and grandmothers had survival value for the human race.

That was true not only of the Cro-Magnon people, those handsome fellows with the high foreheads and the well-shaped chins and the athletic stance, whom we like to think of as our direct ancestors some forty thousand years ago. It was true also of the Neanderthalers, who go back a couple of hundred thousand years and maybe more. Never mind their brutish looks, their short-legged stocky bodies and faces with gorilla brows and no chins. They, too, looked after their old folks. (They also buried their dead, sometimes with flowers.)

We have the evidence, in the remains of a family that was killed and buried by a rock fall in their cave. It happened that grandmother was not at home at the time, but grandfather was. He was too crippled with arthritis to walk a step, and his teeth were gone. But obviously the family cared for him, brought him his food, even chewed the tough, gamey, half-raw meat for him. They must have, to keep him alive.

That old man may have been fifty years old, a remarkably advanced age in those days and long past physical usefulness to the family. Ironically, remembering the slogan of our young people not so long ago, "old" in Stone Age times meant literally anyone over thirty. The average life span was rather less than that, what with the hard, dangerous life, the hunting accidents, the unpredictable food supply. Stone Age people lived on the slippery edge of survival, and there had to be a reason for sharing their food with people too old to hunt or gather wild roots and grains.

One of the reasons was the fire, which required tending. The Neanderthal people still did not know how to start a fire, only to bring brands from a tree struck by lightning or a spontaneous forest fire, and keep it going. Life depended on the fire in Ice Age Europe. But the young men who were out hunting all day and the young women who went food-gathering could not stay awake to tend the fire. That was for the old ones, who, being old, could sleep lightly and wake often in the night. The fire was magic, a powerful spirit with a life of its own, and the old men and women who kept it alive, and carried it in a hollow stone from winter cave to summer camp and back, became endowed with some of its magic.

The old ones had a practical value besides. Out of his long

experience, grandfather was a repository of hunting wisdom, animal lore, weather signs, weapon-making, on which the young men could draw while they sat around the fire. Grandmother was undoubtedly the first babysitter, minding the babies and toddlers who would otherwise be an added burden on the backs of the young women while they scoured the woods and meadows for edible plants, insects, and small animals that could be killed with a stone.

Grandmother had her own store of wisdom. She knew how to help the women in childbirth, bind up wounds, find the herbs that cooled fever and relieved pain. Who else was there but grandmother to pass on the knowledge that an aching, burning swelling could be packed with cooling mud, one of the first remedies known to man, as the medical historians tell us? Or that chewing willow bark helped the pain? Willow bark contains the same acetylsalicylic acid as your aspirin tablet, and it is one of the ancient natural medicines that prehistoric grandmothers knew all about.

Grandmother the herb woman went on into history as the humble doctor of the poor, in those eras when only the rich and noble could afford a physician. We see her in medieval woodcuts, hooded and bent, gathering her healing plants under the right phase of the moon. Sometimes, alas, her wisdom proved fatal for her, and she was stoned or burned as a witch and buried at a crossroads with a stake through her heart to keep her from rising and doing further mischief. Witchcraft, white or black, is also part of our grandmotherly heritage.

Grandmothers have had their place in every known human culture since history began. In American Indian legend it was often the grandmother who reared the epic hero, gave him his weapons, taught him the arts he then taught to his people —like Hiawatha's grandmother, Nokomis. Today, in a very changed world, Indian grandmothers still teach their people's traditions to their grandchildren.

Grandmothers have sometimes been domineering and powerful, as in the traditional Chinese family. I have watched Chinese grandmothers watching their grandchildren in a New York City playground, looking strangely modern in their traditional black trousers and pajamalike tops. The tradition they keep alive seems to me a humane and gentle one. Power is not, or at least need not be, one of our aspirations today. But wisdom and gentleness surely are.

A Look in the Mirror

In the press we have been described as "swingers," "go-go"—deplorable epithets that only a headline writer can love. They do not fit the large majority of us. Nor do the cartoon versions that picture us as ringers for Auntie Mame with the hair and the earrings and the long cigarette holder of the 1920s. That isn't me or any of the grandmothers I have been talking to, although I don't mean we can't still do a pretty fair Charleston.

What the headlines and the cartoons are telling us is that we are younger, slimmer, more concerned with how we look, and almost certainly more involved with the world around us than the conventional image of a grandmother. Statistically that is true. Not only our years but our good years have been substantially extended. A friend of mine who had just turned fifty looked at herself in the mirror and said, "I don't think women used to look like this at fifty, do you?"

She was slim and trim in her well-fitted pants (without girdle, mind you), her skin was fresh and almost unlined, and she still does a hard day's skiing, driving, or manual labor in her house and garden, without any aftereffects that a good night's sleep doesn't cure. I remember her mother at fifty, on a ladder with a paint brush, painting a ceiling. So perhaps the new grandmother is not so very new. But think back one more generation, and the grandmother of today is indeed a new phenomenon.

What is perhaps truly new is the way we see ourselves. Grandmotherhood comes as an enhancement, but not as an exclusive way of life, supplanting all other interests. It is not any longer a signal of age approaching or already arrived. If a woman married and had her first child before she was twenty, and if her eldest followed her example, she can be a grandmother before she is forty.

Whatever our chronological age, whether forty or sixty, it no longer determines the way we spend our days. Some of us still have children growing up at home when our grandchildren begin to come along. Some of us are family women, proud of making a good home life, keeping a husband well and happy while he is still on the job and joining him in an active life of leisure when he retires. Some of us are back in school, studying for a postponed degree or simply for our own expanded knowledge and interests. Some of us are business women, professional women, or volunteers in every kind of community service.

We are also women who happen to have grandchildren.

There are some of us, still, who make their children's families the center of their lives. The family service people think so, and shake an admonitory finger at us. The grandmothers they know seem to be either sad and dependent, or bossy and interfering. Some daughters and daughters-in-law voice the same complaint. "What she'd really like," one is quoted as saying of her children's widowed grandmother, "is to move in and take care of the children and send me out to work."

I don't know how many of us are like that. But however

many there are, they are not making much of their lives. Every city, town, neighborhood has enough useful work that needs doing, and no money to pay for it, to keep all its grandmothers busy every waking hour. No woman who has her health, is not raising children, and doesn't have to work for a living, needs to have time on her hands. There is an old saying that goes, If you want something done, find a busy person to do it. I would add a corollary. If you want to see a good grandmother, look for a busy one. I don't see any future for grandmothers who hang around with nothing on their minds but grandmothering.

And I do not believe they are typical any longer. I have no statistics to prove this—I only report what I see. I see that women who still live through their children are quick to deny that they do. They are either not aware of it or not proud of it. It is no longer the thing to do. Women have too many other ways of using the precious new gift of health and energy in the second half of their lives.

Old Style and New

Take the matter of services. For those young parents who raise their children practically around the corner from the grandparents' home, grandmother is on the spot to help with the new baby, to take the children when their mother has shopping or a doctor or dentist appointment downtown. Grandmother looks after the youngest when the older ones need to be taken somewhere. She babysits when the parents want an evening out. She may take the children for a week-end or a week so that the parents can go on a trip.

There are grandmothers who give a daughter or daughter-in-law a regular day off once a week, either in their own house or in the children's house—a needed break, surely, for the mother of young children, and a valuable help to one who does part-time work at home and must keep business appointments from time to time. Such a mother could of course leave the children with a paid babysitter. But grandmother is nearby, and has both the time and the willingness.

Those are traditional grandmother services which a stay-at-home granny who lives nearby can readily give. What about the untraditional grandmother? What kind of services can she perform, if any? Suppose the children live half a continent away? Suppose grandmother has her own busy life, perhaps her own job?

A working grandmother, one whom I have known through the years, so arranged her job when her grandchildren were little that she could leave it for days or weeks at a time, and take over her daughter's household in another city while her daughter joined the children's father on one of his frequent business trips abroad. The children are nearly grown now, and two are away at college. But when this grandmother asked whether she was still needed, the family said No, not really needed, but it was so much fun to have her there when the parents were away—wouldn't she still continue to come?

Another working grandmother spends part of her vacation, by choice, in her son's house, so that her son and daughter-in-law can have a holiday away together—and so that Grandma can have the children all to herself, without the parents. To her that's a really happy vacation.

Then there are the emergencies. A son or son-in-law calls long-distance and says, "Anne is in the hospital with acute appendicitis—they're operating tomorrow." A vision flashes through grandmother's mind, of the three-year-old and the one-year-old frightened and crying. Possibly—probably—their father can cope. But when she asks if he would like her to come out, he doesn't say no. And so the next morning she arranges matters at the office, clears her desk, packs the essentials—perhaps including urgent work—and takes the next plane.

One pair of young parents with whom I discussed this said, "We wouldn't dream of asking her, and neither would our friends. There's always some way to manage." When I asked, "If she volunteers?" they shrugged. "Well . . . but does she know what she's getting into?"

You can be sure she does. Cooking, cleaning, marketing, holding the anxious husband's hand, sharing his conferences with the doctor if complications develop, flying to the hospital when he or a babysitter is at home—and most important of all, keeping the children reassured and their days happy and ordinary.

She will work harder than she has in years, wake at the slightest sound as she did when her own children were young, and keep her anxieties in check as best she can. If there are rubs and irritations with the parents, either the one at home or the one uncomfortably recovering in the hospital, she will strive to keep her cool and get on with the job she came to do.

And when the crisis is over she will go home and put her feet up and think of all the ways she could have done it better. Next time, she will promise herself, keeping her fingers crossed against there being a next time of the same kind.

She may do it again with a divorce emergency. She may do much the same with crises in day care, nursery schools, perhaps also later schooling. Many a grandmother, who cannot or prefers not to take over the day care for a working daughter or daughter-in-law, will scout the available facilities, public or private. She may do a personal investigation of nursery schools, whether or not she is paying the bill, and offer her recommendations. When a child is not thriving in school, public or private, she may take a sharp look around at alternatives, have talks with principals and headmasters and classroom teachers, and contribute an informed report rather than a snap judgment when the question is discussed with the child's parents.

She may do all this, if she chooses. But always with the understanding that if her advice is not followed there is no hard feeling, and if her advice is followed and does not work out, she can accept the failure of her judgment with equal grace.

That's one kind of untraditional grandmother. She is not quite the same as the grandmother who lived nearby, and who came every evening, took the colicky grandchild out of the exhausted mother's arms, and walked and patted and crooned the baby to sleep.

But our untraditional grandmother, who volunteers services of an untraditional kind, is not really all that different. She is simply an updated version.

Full-Time Grandmother

Some grandmothers are not exactly asked but are more or less dragooned into giving services. These are the grandmothers who take over the job of child day care while daughter or daughter-in-law goes out to work.

Surely this is nothing new, only the classic pattern of the extended family, still being followed by the poor and disadvantaged, or the not so poor who are trying by extra diligence to climb to the next economic rung. Day care centers are too few, too expensive, often unsatisfactory, and in some towns and neighborhoods not available at all. A grandmother who takes over the care of the children for a mother who goes to work or to school is making a significant contribution to the young family's self-improvement, if not indeed to its survival as a family.

Many a *babushka* serves this function in the Soviet Union, where all the young and able-bodied are either at school or at work. Some of them never were traditional *babushkas*, but working or professional women themselves, engineers or physicians (usually of the lowest rank) or linguistically gifted Intourist guides, who were obliged to retire at the legally mandatory age and still have many active, useful years to fill.

One is not surprised that a socialist country makes full use of its manpower—or womanpower—even in some old-fashioned grandmotherly ways. But I never thought to discover the same pattern at affluent levels of our capitalist society, until I began investigating for this book.

The first instance I discovered struck me as a Park Avenue–New Yorkish extravaganza, not at all typical. A daughter—or it may have been a daughter-in-law—brought her months-old infant to its grandmother with the announcement that she was registering for medical school with the intention of going on into psychiatry.

Did grandmother realize how many years she was contracting for? Yes, of course, my informant told me, grandmother was no stranger to the professional world and she knew she was taking on what might be a six-year job. To be sure, Granny lived in a Park Avenue duplex and could well afford nannies, nursery schools, private schooling, the lot. But the child would be her day-to-day responsibility all the same.

This was affluent liberalism with a vengeance. Then I began hearing about other cases of the same, not all with the duplex cooperatives and the nannies but not exactly poverty-stricken either. I heard of them in California, in the Southwest, in the Middle West, and several more in the East.

Most often the full-time take-over of a child was the consequence of a divorce, with the children's mother perforce going back to work. Not such an atypical pattern after all, considering the high divorce rate.

Obviously these are stay-at-home grandmothers, women who perhaps have never had jobs or who retired early from the working world, or they would not be available for full-time child care. They seem to take it in stride, even to enjoy having a child or more than one in the house again. To be a mother at grandmother age, and to know that one is doing a useful, indeed a needed job, is no small satisfaction. Yet they do get tired, especially if the children are young, as they did not the first time around. And some of them confess that they look forward to the daughter marrying again and taking the children back into a home of her own.

What would daughter do if her mother were not able to take the children? If, for example, grandmother too were a working woman? They might, of course, pool their resources. But plenty of divorced young working mothers struggle to keep their children, homes, and jobs going at the same time, without grandmotherly help. We all know some of them, and as mothers we feel for their hardships, which are very real. Our society does not give them much if any help. They can be thankful for traditional grandmothers, if their children are lucky enough to have one.

No-Service Grandmother

Most grandmotherly services are voluntary, to offer or not as we like. There are grandmothers who are as generous as any of these others with warmth, time, interest, even money (tactfully contributed)—but not services.

The wise ones make this limitation clear from the start. One I know stated it outright when her first grandchild was born. She said, "I'll pay for babysitters any time you like, but I will not babysit." That grandchild is now in college, and there are a total of four more in two families. But she has never been asked to take over even in an emergency, and there has never been the slightest resentment of her position. How could there be, when there is constant evidence of her love and concern for the grandchildren, and their parents as well, in a dozen other ways?

It was, in fact, the parents of one of her sets of grandchildren who protested at the beginning of this discussion that they would never ask grandmother to step in, whatever the emergency. They genuinely respect her privacy and her preference for how she will use her time, and they love her no less for it.

Perhaps that is the newest style in grandmothers, newer than the kind who, busy as she may be with job or profession or a full life of her own, will drop everything at a moment's notice and fly to the rescue.

Freedom of choice is one of the nicest fringe benefits of grandmotherhood. It is no longer a question of how to be a good grandmother. We have the choice of what kind of good grandmother we want to be.

We do not have to buy the parents of our grandchildren with services. No good comes of letting oneself be used. Exploitation, of grandmothers or anyone else, breeds only resentment in the exploited, and guilt—hence resentment again—in the exploiter. We earn love and respect for *not* doing as much as for doing, as long as we make the limits of our involvement clear.

Perhaps for the first time in our lives, when we are grandmothers we no longer have to do anything we don't want to do. The choices are our own.

Grandmother on Horseback

At a time when the Indian fires made a wall that blossomed and faded at night on three sides of the sky, this grandmother was known as one of the best horsewomen in Kansas.

They were used to seeing her riding with a sunbonnet on her head—not in pants, but with wide skirts hullabalooing out behind her in the wind. . . .

She could stuff a cod very nicely, stitch up its belly, and see that it baked. From the French side she learned to put fresh mackerel in kegs with white wine and lemon peel and a bouquet of spice. But on these occasions her beautiful red hair would be pulled back from her face, tied tight into a net at the back of her head, as naturally as if it had itself recoiled in distaste from the monotony of the tasks performed before it.

—"Episode in the Life of an Ancestor," by Kay Boyle

3

Building Bridges

We were sitting under the trees on the New England campus of our college, enjoying a quiet interval during class reunion. We were all of an age, most of us grandmothers, and the talk turned naturally to grandchildren, when one of my classmates burst out suddenly, almost tearfully, "I have a five-year-old grandson who doesn't even know he has a grandmother!"

Her deprivation is simply one of geography. She lives on the East Coast, her daughter on the West Coast, and a whole continent lies between. It is a deprivation many of us share.

To a grandmother with both money and leisure, distance may present no obstacle to frequent trips back and forth. Plenty of grandmothers can afford not only their own trips but presents of air fare to the young families, just to see the grandchildren as often as possible.

But in our day many of us are still working at jobs and professions, and many of our daughters and daughters-in-law are also working, so that even when there is enough money for travel there is often not enough time. The long, leisurely visits of past generations, often lasting for months, are no longer possible for us, quite apart from whether they are desirable in today's world of untraditional family relationships.

To know a child and have a child know us we need to spend time together, and at frequent intervals, especially during the early years when they are growing and changing almost from day to day. Many of us have experienced that painful moment when the child who clambered into our lap at one year shies away from us as from a stranger at two.

How to bridge the gap?

My own solution was born of desperation. My grandchildren were three and one when I began sending them picture postcards—of skyscrapers, bridges, airplanes, the Statue of Liberty, when I was at home in New York—"This is how I flew home" and "This is where I live." In between times I sent them pictures of birds, small animals, boats, trains, almost anything that a young child can identify (my husband began to send them museum cards of paintings and sculptures, an early start on sharing one of *his* interests). Instead of a signature, because they were still a long way from reading, although I cannot draw a line even with a ruler I managed a silly caricature of my face, recognizable only by the earrings. (Here I cribbed from my husband, who draws a mustache, glasses, and a pipe.)

The next time I came to their Rocky Mountain home to visit, they got out a shoebox in which they had kept all the cards, and we sat on the floor and looked at them together. There was no longer any question about whether they knew their grandmother. What was still more rewarding, Aviva began writing to me, first in pictures of her own, soon with her own wavery signature in block capitals accompanied by strings of HHH and XXX. These days, at seven, she writes me letters, and Jonathan at four and a half has begun our correspondence with pictures.

(I told this postcard story to my distressed classmate, and the next time we met in the Alumnae House she was picking out a postcard to send to her grandson in San Francisco.)

A mother tells me that her child began receiving little packages from Grandma when the child was eighteen months old, and for a long time the little girl assumed that every package that came to the house was for her, from Granny, until she was able to make out her own initial, B for Belinda, on the address. The packages contained nothing expensive or important, just whatever small objects the grandmother had happened to pick up or put together that might please a young child. I remember that one contained a number of empty sewing thread spools (that grandmother was a needlewoman) strung together in graduated sizes on a bright-colored cord. To Belinda what made the little things important was that they were her very own, addressed directly to her.

Grandma Books

Another grandmother sent her grandson little books she made herself, the pages stapled or stitched together and pasted up with picture postcards, snapshots, cutouts, with captions and a slender running story printed in block letters for a beginning reader. Each little book was a record of a visit—"This is what we did when you were here at Easter" or "This is about when I came to see you at Christmas."

This grandmother has no pretensions to artistic or literary skill—by profession she is a registered nurse. She merely put together for the boy whatever bits and pieces she had kept as souvenirs of an experience they had shared. The proof of the grandson's pleasure in these books is that he has treasured them all, side by side with his favorite storybooks, on his own bookshelf.

There is almost no end to the possible subjects for homemade Grandmother books. They can be biographical—"This is about you when you were a baby," and "This is about when Mommy (or Daddy) was your age." Or true adventure stories about trips and experiences, her own, Grandpa's, or of Tommy's father or mother before Tommy was born. And they are all guaranteed to fascinate the particular reader to whom they are addressed, because they are made for him and about him, and no one else.

Many of us find pleasure in travel in these years, and one young granddaughter showed her grandmother a way to share a trip. Grandmother had made a journey around the world. With her young people at home always in mind, she had sent postcards and descriptive letters all along the way, and she brought back pictures and small mementoes that she could carry from all the lands she had visited, not only as presents but to make her account of her travels the more graphic to her children and grandchildren.

The first sign of success in her effort to share her trip was an invitation from her eldest granddaughter to come to school and give a talk about it to the child's third grade class. The next, she learned, was that granddaughter had put it all down in a storybook, written, illustrated, and bound by her own hand, with the title, "My Trip Around the World with Grandma."

I recently learned that a commercial company makes books about a particular child. A relative who wants to give one as a gift fills out a questionnaire about the child, and for a fee the company prints a little storybook embodying the information. To me this commercialized (or "personalized," as the delusive advertising euphemism has it) exploitation of a child's delight in stories about himself or herself is a poor match for the genuinely personal product of our own hands, however inexpert.

Granny Historian

And what better use is there for the snapshots and memorabilia we all hoard, whether of the grandchild himself or of his mother or father who was once our own child? Older children enjoy poring over Grandma's family album. They laugh over the postures and fashions of long ago. But they also ask questions that reveal their longing for a sense of continuity with the family's past.

This longing recurs periodically through the growing years, each time at a new level of interest. In my explorations with grandmothers and grandchildren for this book I have come across repeated instances of it even in grown children. A young man in his twenties asked his mother to write down for him everything she could tell him about his grandmother and the great-aunts and great-uncles whom he dimly remembered from childhood. He wanted to know about their life in the "old country," how and why they had come to America, how they had lived here, what they had been like as a family, as individuals. She showed me a copy of the letter she wrote him, and I could see what a rich recreation of his origins this must have been for him, and what a record this will be for his children, my friend's grandchildren, when they are old enough to be interested. It was a recreation for her too as she wrote it, bringing together all the lively vignettes she had stored away in her memories of her own childhood and the grown-ups who had peopled it.

Another young man, this one in his thirties, brought notebook and pen along on a visit to his eighty-year-old aunt and her sister of seventy-eight. He kept the two of them going for hours in salty reminiscences of their parents—his grandparents, whom he had never known—of the houses they had lived in, the way the city was in those days, the joys and griefs of that vanished family world. They gave him a picturesque vision of his grandfather as a young railroad man who had taken part in the building of the railroad in the Northwest before they and his father were born, and told him stories of that adventurous life they remembered hearing in their own childhood. He duly noted it all down in his notebook, with an interest that never flagged, and vowed to come back for more.

A young child's interest is still very narrow. He is still the center of his universe, and what he can grasp must be small in scope and revolving around himself. Here is where a judicious grandmotherly selection from her box of souvenirs, chosen just for him, will meet with a joyful welcome. And it cannot but strengthen those threads we spin across time and distance to our grandchildren.

Unbirthday Surprises

Phone calls, no matter how frequent, are not enough. A disembodied voice has small meaning for a young child. Cards and packages for birthdays, Christmas, Easter, are also not enough. For one thing, they meet with too much competition for the child's attention on those standard occasions when everybody sends something. No, if we must build our bridges with postage stamps, we must make them *unbirthday* occasions, as Alice called them in Wonderland—the nicest kind, said Alice. They must come as surprises, with no excuse except a wish to write something or send something for our own pleasure and the child's.

If we are lucky, our grandchildren will begin responding in kind with pictures of their own, crayoned on a rainy day, then with letters as soon as they learn to write. Some grandmothers send the child a box of children's writing paper to encourage this next step. In our era of long-distance telephones and flying visits the art of letter-writing may have declined, but who knows? The urge of loving grandmothers to build airmail bridges to their distant grandchildren may yet revive it!

And if we like to think of ourselves as contributing to our grandchildren's education, there is no doubt at all that cards and letters and homemade books from Grandma, addressed directly to himself and herself, will incidentally spur the child's appetite for learning to read and write.

The Child We Cannot Know

Not all our grandchildren are equally responsive to us, nor we to them. Sometimes it is because we have not found an opportunity to know the child. But it is also true—as some of us have discovered with one among our own children—that there are individual differences which make it harder to communicate with, or to be with, one child than with another. This has nothing to do with our love or concern for the child. The chemistry is somehow wrong.

A grown granddaughter told me how she once was sent to stay with her grandmother in another city when she was four, and she was so unhappy that one morning she packed her little bag, stole out of the house, and got on the first bus. She had no idea what bus to take. She simply knew that she had come on a bus and a bus would take her home. (Of course she was quickly found and delivered safely back home.)

A young child, or even an older one, may be merely homesick, and unable to tell us so. If that is so, it is clearly grandma's job to find out, and not take the child's longing for home as a rejection of herself. We can remember being homesick, too, even when we were with people who were kind and loving. But this young woman remembered with poignant clarity that she really had not *liked* her grandmother.

Years later she came to understand how much it had grieved her grandmother that she had been unable to establish some rapport with the little girl. It is not easy in any case to make friends with a four-year-old. That's a cautious, rather standoffish age, and this little girl seems to have been a particularly shy child. I suspect that grandmother, too, was shy, and to compensate for it she may have been too aggressive in approaching the child. Making friends with children, especially young ones, is rather like making friends with a cat. We must make no sudden movements or loud sounds, or the cat flees—and the child shrinks inside himself. With the child as with the cat, we must figuratively put out a hand and let him come to us when he is ready.

Sometimes even that does not work. We may wait and wait patiently, and put out our tentative feelers, and still the child does not come to us. We may have to accept the fact that one or another of our grandchildren may never be our friend.

Or it may happen, in a year, two years, when the child arrives at another level of growth and new aspects of the personality unfold. We cannot make a child love us. We can only give love, and hope that some day love will come in return.

That Feeling of Safety

After I reached the age of fourteen, my grandmother's intellectual limitations became trying to me, and her Puritan morality began to seem to me to be excessive; but while I was a child her great affection for me, and her intense care for my welfare, made me love her and gave me that feeling of safety that children need. I remember when I was about four or five years old lying awake thinking how dreadful it would be when my grandmother was dead. When she did in fact die, which was after I was married, I did not mind at all. But in retrospect, as I have grown older, I have realized more and more the importance she had in moulding my outlook on life. Her fearlessness, her public spirit, her contempt for convention, and her indifference to the opinion of the majority have always seemed good to me and have impressed themselves upon me as worthy of imitation. She gave me a Bible with her favorite texts written on the fly-leaf. Among these was "Thou shalt not follow a multitude to do evil." Her emphasis upon this text led me in later life not to be afraid of belonging to small minorities.

—*The Autobiography of Bertrand Russell*

4

They Get Older

As our grandchildren get on into the middle childhood years our connections with them often seem to be breaking off. The little girl and boy who used to spend hours with us in the kitchen, the playground, the zoo, now have other ways to spend their time. They would rather be with their schoolmates, their best friends, or watching a favorite television program which grandmother's phone call too often interrupts.

And if they do consent to come to the telephone they no longer want to chatter on about what they did yesterday or what they are going to do tomorrow—we no longer have power to charm. They are likely to say, "Excuse me, Grandma, I have to do something now, goodbye," and we are left holding the phone, feeling somehow pushed out of the child's life.

And of course, for the time being, we are. So are their parents. The children are finding their pathways out into the world, and it is no use trying to cling to the bond we had with them a year or two years ago. Still, if we have built a fairly sound bridge to them until now, they will come back. Indeed they are likely to keep coming back time after time, reopening communications with us each time on a new level.

One of these times may be in the early teens, when questions of large importance begin to concern them. In these years they begin to worry about themselves, about how they are doing, about the kind of people they are growing up to be. Childhood is receding behind them, and the future, looming dark and mysterious ahead, seems teeming with changes to come, choices to be made. They face it with both longing and foreboding, reaching forward, pulling back, like the waves of an incoming tide. And it is of course a kind of tide that is rising in them, a tide of growth that is pushing them to think about the choice of a career, about love affairs and sex, about marriage and children. If there has been a death in the family, they are almost surely thinking about grownups they love, about people getting old, about sickness and death.

They may come to us wanting to talk about these heavy subjects that sometimes, for whatever reasons, they find hard to discuss with their parents. Or perhaps they talk about them with Mom and Dad and come and talk about them with Grandma and Grandpa as well. Some of these are sensitive subjects for us, especially that last one. We may have avoided thinking overmuch about our own future years.

But for our grandchildren we gather up our forces and give them our life's harvest of wisdom and philosophy. In the effort to give good and comforting answers to the young questioners whom we love, we very often arrive at good and comforting answers for ourselves.

"*Mother Is So Hard-Hearted!* . . ."

These are also the years in which they are trying to establish their independence of their parents, and what they bring to us is often a list of complaints. "Dad is so unreasonable about letting me do this . . ." "Mother is so hard-hearted about that..." "They just can't seem to understand!..." The specifics may not be the same as when our children were young adolescents, or when we were. But the theme is the same, with variations.

This is when our wisdom, if not indeed our love, is put to the test. A cardinal rule when they were younger—you had it said to you and have said it to yourself—is not to criticize a parent's handling of the child in front of the child. Here you have the child without the parent, and the child is tacitly inviting you to conspire with him or her against the parent. And that, too, is against grandmotherly rules.

Yet the last thing you want to do is shake the child's trust in you as a refuge, if not an ally, against all the world including parents.

Some of the complaints are easily answered. Why is mother so absolutely livid when Richard doesn't come home at the time he said he would? Nothing happened to him! He and his friend just stopped in for a hamburger, and they met another friend, and they went over to that friend's house... and so on.

This is your chance to explain parents to their child, and perhaps to give the child a somewhat more mature attitude to his parents. You can easily justify a mother's anxiety when a child fails to come home and fails to phone. You've been there yourself during your own parenthood.

It's no mystery why Rickie didn't phone. He didn't just forget, or fail to find a dime or a phone booth. He simply preferred not to give his mother the opportunity to say no to whatever he was up to, and order him home at once. On the other hand, he can perfectly well be made to understand what a peculiar kind of cruelty it is to leave a parent unknowing and anxious. No matter how sure he is that there is nothing for her to worry about—nothing can happen to him!—his mother does worry, and he is a big enough boy to be considerate of her worrying whether or not he thinks it is justified. And perhaps she has something to worry about, in a big confused world where accidents can happen and where not every adult is to be trusted.

Even if he doesn't agree, he can do the one little thing that allays her worry. He can telephone. It's a rule that children have to learn, the younger the better. Their following or not following it affects not only their parents but ourselves, their grandmothers. There was a night in my own life that I will never forget, not as a grandmother but as a great-aunt. My great-niece and her roommate, both freshmen in a college near New York, were coming into the city to go to the theater and sleeping over in my apartment. When they were not home at midnight I began walking the floor. At twelve-thirty I was climbing the wall. At one o'clock I called the police. The thought of two eighteen-year-old girls somewhere around Times Square in the small hours of the morning is pure nightmare.

At one-fifteen the girls came in safe and sound (they had merely stopped to eat) just as the big gray-haired policeman and his younger partner arrived. The big one, obviously a father, listened to the girls' story, and then pointed a finger at them. "The only thing you did wrong," he said, "was not phoning."

Do We Interfere?

Most of the children's complaints about their parents are readily answered on the grounds of parents' love and responsibility, which children must come to understand, however irksome they find the resulting restraints. But what if we agree with the child in finding the parent unfair, "hard-hearted"? Or if something in the parent's handling of a situation seems to us downright unwise? What do we say to the child?

Nothing, in my rulebook, except to explain and palliate if we can. If we feel strongly about the matter, the only person we can discuss it with is the parent.

This comes under the heading of giving unasked advice, something that in our mature years we must surely have learned not to do. But for a grandchild's sake we may chance it.

A grandmother among my friends had such a situation to deal with. The complaint came not from the young teen-age granddaughter, but from her older sister, a levelheaded college junior, who felt that her young sibling was being allowed more freedom than was good for her. Grandmother had felt the same, but had hesitated to interfere, until the older girl expressed the same anxiety. The child was spirited and headstrong—her father, with some pride, called her "independent." Older sister, who felt she knew the world, said, "Daddy and Mother just don't realize what Cissy's getting into.

"I've been away from home for three years now," she went on, "and I couldn't possibly do anything my parents wouldn't approve of. I've talked to them about Cissy. I wish you would too."

So grandmother talked to them. She aimed her comments especially at Daddy, her son-in-law, whose relationship with the younger girl was particularly close, and with whom Grandma herself is on extremely good terms—not by chance, but as one of the rewards of good grandmothering. She spoke forthrightly, as is her way, and Cissy's indulgent Daddy as well as her mother took Grandma's criticism in good part—for one thing, because it was thoughtful criticism and had the ring of truth.

What she mainly told her daughter and son-in-law was that they had somehow not made the guidelines for conduct in the outside world as clear for their younger daughter as they had for the older one. And they acknowledged that, as happens not infrequently with the children who come after the firstborn, they had taken a good deal for granted, and had not made the same conscious effort to clarify their values to their second child as they had to their first.

How effective this grandmother's intervention may be in the parents' future handling of Cissy remains to be seen. But it seemed to me a good example for us all, in how to give unasked advice about a grandchild—and make it acceptable.

Not easy, no. As our grandchildren get older, our part in their lives calls for ever more delicate handling.

Our success in such an effort depends very much on the relationship we have built with the grandchildren and their parents in the years before. And it depends, too, on how carefully—up to that moment—we have followed our grandmotherly option of *not* interfering. The more sparing we have been with our unasked advice, the more carefully we are listened to when we do offer it.

The Inside Story

There is another way in which I believe we can pass on wisdom to our grandchildren. Grandparents are always being told that their role is to provide continuity, and of course that is so. To our grandchildren, what we tell them about their parents' childhood and our own young years is living history.

I think there is something more that we as grandmothers can do as our grandsons and granddaughters enter into their adolescent years groping for a road of their own. There is a deeper side to our memories of when Daddy and Mommy were growing up, and I believe we can share that, too. I see it as a kind of psychological history, a contribution we can make to our grandchildren's understanding not only of their parents, but also of themselves and their management of their own relationships later on.

I am speaking of the inside story, the more inward levels of our relationship with our own child, our grandchild's parent, during our motherhood years. A grandchild's complaints about mother or father, our own daughter or son, inevitably stir some of our own uneasy memories about ourselves as mothers. Which of us doesn't still harbor some regret about mistakes we made, or think we made, not to mention a sneaking suspicion that there were a great many more errors we don't even know we made?

Someone has said that it is no wonder grandparents and grandchildren get along so well—they have a common enemy. Obviously we and our grandchildren have the same target for our displeasure—your mother my daughter, your father my son. But our grandchildren also hear some complaints about ourselves. Our grown child voices many criticisms of us as parents. Husband and wife complain to each other about their mothers (and fathers), and children, who are the world's most accomplished eavesdroppers, hear a great deal more of this than they let on. Sometimes a parent criticizes us directly to the child, either about the past—"When I was your age, Grandma used to . . ."—or the present, "I wish Grandma would . . ." or wouldn't, as the case may be.

Children rarely carry this sort of comment back to us, at least not openly. But it colors their thinking and feeling about the relationship between parent and child, and it may actually trouble them.

Knowing this, and knowing that we did indeed sometimes behave with our own children as we now wish we hadn't, would it not be a good thing, now and then, to talk openly about our mistakes of the past? Especially with a grandchild with whom we have a relationship of trust and intimacy? And especially when we hear echoes, as so often we do, of our own parent days in a grandchild's complaint about Mommy or Daddy? Don't our past conflicts with a son or daughter come back to haunt us in these intimate sessions with a grandchild? Don't they even sound like a replay of the old tussles?

Our grandmothers and perhaps our mothers were not so aware as we are of their mistakes in child-rearing, or we think they were not. They had the support of tradition in their time as mothers. But we belong to a generation that questioned many traditions. The revolution in child psychology was in full swing when we were young mothers, and many of us took courses and read books—Dr. Spock, at least—about how to be good parents.

More than once we felt the ground shaking under our feet. What was the right thing to do about feeding, about toilet training, about bedtime? Could we trust our mother's advice, when so-and-so with a resounding Ph.D. after his or her name told us to do just the opposite? And didn't some of us in our time have head-to-head battles with our mothers about these crucial matters? As for the adolescent years, everyone was telling us what and what not to do, and that argument is still going on.

Right or wrong in the end, we were surely made conscious of child-rearing methods and philosophies, and conscious, too, of our own shortcomings. There was a lot of amateur psychologizing going on, which now in our mature years we rather discount. Psychologizing, ideologizing—no intellectual generalizations about children have the weight of direct perception and experience with an individual child. Plus a spot of common sense.

But there is no question that as grandmothers we still have

that awareness and that interest in the emotional development of children, most acutely of our grandchildren, in whom we have an investment of love and concern.

A grandmother today can be very much aware that she had difficulties with her daughter or son, and that a grandchild has heard or felt intimations of this. And a grandmother is far enough away now from that stage of her life to look back at it with some detachment. She may be able to acknowledge to herself, at least, that she didn't treat the kid all that well! A grandmother can afford to admit that her son or daughter has had legitimate complaints against her.

Suppose you had one of these bright twelve-, thirteen-, fourteen-year-olds visiting you, your granddaughter, curious about things, shaking things up inside herself, and maybe at that point having plenty of complaints about her mother, your daughter. In that atmosphere, suppose you found that you could confess some of your doubts about your own handling of similar situations with your daughter, her mother. And thrash out the pros and cons with the child, as far as the child seems able to grasp them. Might that not be a wholesome experience for both of you?

A child who has had a good dose of criticisms of Grandma, direct or indirect, might welcome such an airing with relief. And perhaps it may improve the atmosphere between the girl and her mother at least a little, in the way that new light tends to change a focus or an attitude.

At some point in their growth, children relinquish the vision of parents as all-powerful gods, and begin to see them as human beings with human limitations. In the adolescent years they tend to swing to the other extreme, and say (although usually they don't wholly believe) that their parents don't know *anything*, that a mother or father is wrong about almost *everything*. A touch of grandmotherly self-criticism, judiciously injected, can help to give more balance to this teen-age image of parents, can help a child achieve a little tolerance of human individuality and its limitations.

Such confidences need not be limited to granddaughters about mothers, although they seem the easiest. Granddaughters about fathers, and grandsons about either parent, can equally benefit from such an exploration.

There are many caveats. The one about psychologizing, for example. The kind of pseudo-Freudian interpretations some of us used to indulge in are archaic today, and some of the succeeding psychological theories that had great vogue now seem equally irrelevant. In any event they have no place in conversation with a child.

We need to use discretion in our choice of words, and to avoid any chance characterizations of parents that a child may misunderstand, or may grasp as a weapon against a parent in a moment of heated conflict—"even Grandma said you were . . ." We cannot look for any magical new dawning in the relationship between grandchild and parent, parent and grandmother—changes come, but not instantly, and not uniformly. And we do well to listen, perhaps even more than we talk.

A grown granddaughter gave me the perfect summing up for this occasional opening of inner chambers with our grandchildren. She said, "Whatever else it may do for them now, it's bound to be a help to them for their next thirty years." Amen.

The Sabbath Visit

Grandma Minde was a tall well-groomed woman, neat and pious to a fault. Her special concern was to make sure that her grandchildren grew up to be observant, God-fearing Jews. So she moistened the tips of her fingers with her tongue and straightened the boys' earlocks; she dusted and smoothed out their clothes and heard their prayers morning, noon, and night. In return for all this, it was obligatory for the boys to visit her every Saturday afternoon to wish her good Sabbath. They sat along the wall and decorously awaited their "Sabbath treat." No one received too much of the "Sabbath treat" but it was served on clean, shining plates. The treat usually consisted of a small apple and a peach and a piece of carob and either a fig, or several withered raisins. Along with the treat came interminable lectures. From these lectures one gathered that one must obey one's parents and indeed all God-fearing people, that it was most important to be a good Jew, and, if you weren't God would punish you. . . .

When the moment came to say goodbye, she kissed each child in turn, as only a mother can, and wept, as only a mother can weep. And when we had climbed into the wagon and the journey had begun, she called to the children, "Goodbye, children! God grant that you all live to attend my funeral!"

—*The Great Fair: Scenes from My Childhood,*
by Sholem Aleichem

5

Visiting

A friend of mine flies across the continent, literally from coast to coast, to see her grandchildren. She does it several times a year, and she is made gloriously welcome not only by her daughter, her son-in-law, the children, but all their friends. She has a ball every time she goes. But she never stays more than a week, and often only four or five days. She waves goodbye to a chorus of pleas that she stay a little longer, but she goes nevertheless. She says, "They love me more when they see less of me."

Another grandmother told me of visiting her son and daughter-in-law in another city. They have built her a separate little apartment, bed-sitting room and bath, over the garage which is attached to the house, and it is reached through a door at the end of the upstairs hall. She was in her apartment one afternoon when she heard steps outside her door, and was about to open it when she paused. An interesting conversation was going on beyond the door, between her teen-age granddaughter and a girlfriend.

Said the friend, "How absolutely super! You have a place to keep your grandmother locked up! Ours is always sitting in the living room—you can never get her out."

"Why would you want to get her out?" asked granddaughter.

"Oh, you know how it is—you can't bring your boyfriend in, can't play the hi-fi, can't turn on the programs you want on the TV—grandmothers never like the same things you do!"

How much do we really enjoy visiting our married children and their families? How much do they *really* enjoy having us? Yes, I hear the protestations from both sides. We make the same protestations in my family.

And how is it when they visit us? Some families, who live nearby, make a ritual weekly visit to grandmother's. She cooks and bakes and everyone gets up from the table feeling stuffed and somnolent, except perhaps the teen-age grandchildren, whose inner space seems never to be filled. Yet no one, least of all grandmother, would think of altering either the ritual visit or any of its rites, including the too ample meal.

When families live far apart the ritual is limited rather to the family holidays—Thanksgiving, Christmas—and it is the same ritual in even larger dimensions. "Over the river and through the woods," we sing, calling up visions of a different world, to our eyes a much warmer, closer world of family pleasures than our own. We stuff ourselves with the roast turkey, the mince and pumpkin pies, in celebration, or perhaps in memoriam. The traditional meal is about the only part of that world that we can recreate on the holiday visits nowadays. Or possibly that world of joyful family feeling existed only in the lithographs and the engravings. The traditional picture we cherish may never have been the reality.

On the other hand, the family visit of those days could well have supplied the emotional as well as culinary satisfactions that we imagine. The grown and married children were indeed returning to their childhood home, recreating for their children the frolics and follies of their young years in the same setting. For their part, the grandparents were not only younger in years but more accustomed to physical exertions than we are today. And the family home was big and roomy, its walls attuned to the noise of flocks of romping children.

A modern grandmother calls me on the telephone. "Well, they've gone," she says in an exhausted voice. Her children and grandchildren have been visiting her, crammed together in her modern apartment with its one bedroom and tiny kitchen, sleeping on the convertible sofa, on an air mattress on the floor, on a roll-away bed, and the baby in a rented crib. How was it? I ask. "Glorious!" she says. And then she adds plaintively, "How can it be that I love them so much, am so glad to have them come—and so glad to see them go?"

And another grandmother, equally devoted, confesses, "I don't know why it is, but sooner or later on every visit there is an explosion between my daughter and me, and I vow I will never visit them again or have them visit me. And of course it is all over the next morning, and we are both sorry and maybe we cry a little—because, you know, we really do love each other very much, and we even understand each other rather well. And yet, there it is."

We all insist we enjoy these visits to the hilt. We insist, and sincerely, that we would never dream of giving them up. And a grandmother will confess to no one, except perhaps another grandmother, how hard it really is, how often there are feelings of strain, of irritation, of fatigue—and how often, as we and they wave goodbye, we are left with a residue of disappointment, of things done and not done, of feelings ruffled and expectations unfulfilled.

But we will never, no, never, abandon these ritual visits.

I propose to look into this deceptive phenomenon, even at the risk of deflating the myth of family bliss that we all cling to. Perhaps by taking a cool look at it we can find the worm in the apple, not just half the worm. If we know what the stresses are, we may be able to ease them a little, and make our visits more like our anticipation of them.

No doubt our anticipation is partly to blame for disappointments. We prepare for our going or their coming in the highest spirits, especially if visits are few and far between. We give never a thought to old rubs and chronic irritations. We look forward to nothing but joy in meeting and being together—because it is true, we do love them and we believe they love us.

But when we are together we are the same people we always were. Love does not transform us, or them. Nor does the joy of being with them make us wiser or more tolerant toward each other than we have been in the past. As one daughter said of her inevitable run-ins with her mother, "That's what is. We both blow our stacks, she and I. But I do love her and it doesn't matter."

So perhaps the first axiom for making it a good visit is not to expect a perfect one.

The Forgetting Hormone

The mind is a seducer and a deceiver. I think of it as not unlike our other organs, each one busily secreting its juices to contribute to the body's health and well-being. The mind's peculiar juice is psychological rather than chemical, and it is highly selective. I call it the forgetting hormone. We are proud of our powers of remembering, but I don't hear people boasting of their powers of forgetting. Yet a trickle of the mind's forgetting hormones seeps through all our memories, neatly picking out those that give pain, and dimming or expunging them.

The power to forget is a healing balm, but it has its price. We forget the unpleasant aspects of our last family visit long before it is time for the next one, and we anticipate each fresh visit as though we had learned nothing from the one before.

Our memory plays us still meaner tricks than that. We

forget the long-past displeasures we experienced with our grandchildren's parents as children. We forget that our children were noisy, disruptive, destructive, that they could be disobedient, disagreeable, rude, sulky, untidy, unwashed, unmanageable, and downright impossible at times, that they bickered and fought with one another, left their toys and clothes scattered everywhere, lost things, forgot things—that they were, in fact, not painted cherubs but living children.

Our grown children's memories of us may be equally slanted. We weren't always perfect parents. When we see our grandchildren behaving like children, and their parents behaving like parents, we are distressed. We are even more distressed when we find our grown children still behaving toward us like children. And ourselves, who are surely old enough to know better, behaving to them as we did when we were their young parents.

We speak of our grandmotherly detachment, and of course it is part of our new role and status in the second half of life. But it is not by any means all-pervading, and we cannot count on it to sustain us automatically in these encounters with our young families. There is no button marked DETACHMENT that we can push. Try as we may to remain aloof although affectionate, we do become emotionally involved. We do still care, sometimes too much. We cannot always hold our tongues or, saying nothing, avoid expressing our displeasure in face and gesture. And we get into hassles, willy-nilly.

Would we rather duck out of it all? Do we want to cool the relationships, or perhaps step out of them altogether?

Perish forbid! We want to be part of our children's and grandchildren's lives, and have them be part of ours. We feel bereft if we do not see them for too long a time. And so, as usual in life, the choice is not one thing or the other but something in between We will certainly continue to visit them and invite them. But we can try to rearrange our expectations and prepare our attitudes, so as to make the most of a visit's pleasures and the least of its disappointments.

The Big Visit

Whether we go to their house or they come to ours, the big family visit has enormous joys but also some built-in disappointments. We often come away from a Thanksgiving or Christmas gathering, or an anniversary celebration, feeling that we have had no chance really to talk to anybody.

The grandchildren naturally expect to be the center of attention. But when our visits with our grown children have been few and far between, we find ourselves getting into adult talk with them, catching up on their news and ours, all but forgetting the children. And the children, ignored and bored, become obstreperous. And their parents feel obliged to discipline them.

A friend of mine was recalling visits from one of her grandmothers, the one the children called the talking grandmother. Grandmother talked and talked, and granddaughter, who may have been about six, stood on one foot and the other, waiting to speak to her mother. Finally she broke in. "Don't interrupt, dear," said her mother, "wait until Grandma finishes." "But if I wait until Grandma finishes I'll never get to talk!" retorted little Alice. And of course little Alice had to be rebuked for getting fresh in Grandma's presence. Hassle Number One.

A great-grandmother was remembering the Thanksgivings when she was a young grandmother and the clan gathered at her house. After dinner the grown-ups stayed around the table, talking, and the children went upstairs to play. It was a big house with many rooms, ideal for hide-and-seek.

Great-grandmother, reminiscing, said, "They always had such fun!" And one of her grown grandsons interjected, "Yes, that was when Jimmy always beat up Bobby!"

Great-grandmother had forgotten the fights and the inevitable sequence that followed, when one cousin came complaining to his parents about the other, the other's parents had to administer punishment, and someone, child or parent or perhaps both, suffered bruised feelings. Hassle Number Two.

Of course it was funny, but the laughter was nostalgic. With all the brawls and the batterings, those grown children and grandchildren would have given a great deal to have those Thanksgivings back again. The next best thing was to get together and remember.

The big family gathering brings out an aspect of our feelings that we are usually a little ashamed of. There can be no question about it—we have favorites. We had favorites among our own children, however impartial we were in our dealings with them, and we cannot help having favorites among our grandchildren.

With some the reason is geographical. They live nearby, we see them often, and we feel closer to them than to the others because we know them better.

But with some of our grandchildren the reason lies deeper. They reflect the qualities of the newcomers to the family, the sons-in-law and daughters-in-law. However much we try, and however well we succeed (and often we do) in accepting and loving our in-law children, there are always the new, the unfamiliar traits and ways that they bring from their different family background, and in some of the grandchildren these differences stand out conspicuously. We may not actively dislike these differences—it may only be their unfamiliarity that we shy at. Still, it's there, and it comes out strikingly when all the grandchildren are gathered together for the big family party. The words come readily to our minds if not to our lips— "... not like our family...."

We cannot help preferring the familiar, but we can help showing irritation with the unfamiliar. The differences between our own grown child and our in-law child, and the differences among our grandchildren, can become irritants if we are not watchful. And the irritation can lead to an unnecessary confrontation—usually with our own rather than our in-law child—about some unrelated triviality on which our discomfort or disapproval becomes pinned.

Here is a son-in-law who, whatever else his charms and virtues, never eats breakfast. And here is a granddaughter who at five or six is already aping her father and refusing her breakfast. Grandmother, who strongly believes in a proper breakfast for children, says nothing the first morning, nor the second morning. But before the visit has ended she finds herself launched on a lecture to her daughter on child nutrition and a mother's responsibility for instilling good food habits in the children. Hassle Number Three.

Then there is the question of fatigue, ours and theirs. A single big day, a mammoth dinner party for the whole family, is something we can all survive. But if it is a visit from afar and we are to be together for days, then it is another matter. We must take into account that they and we are experiencing a disruption of our daily routines, that we are all accommodating to each other in dozens of small ways, and that no one, old or young, can maintain his best behavior for too long a time.

We become tired, and it is not only because in our grandparent years we are not as young as we were. Our fatigue has to do also with the fact that since our children grew up and left home we have become accustomed to a different life. Our life now is one of relative order and quietness at home, of following our own patterns of social activity alternating with periods of solitude, of living at our own pace instead of at the pace and demands of our children.

We are no longer so accomplished at tuning out the constant coming and going, the running up and down and back and forth, the slamming of doors, the noisy playing, the outbursts of quarreling, fighting, scolding, the tempers and the tears. When we were parents in our own house and the children became too much for us, we could always order them to their own room to play quietly for a while. As grandmothers we do not have that authority, or we are reluctant to exercise it. And we are reluctant to refuse the constant demands on our attention: "Read to me, Grandma!" "Tell me a story, Grandma!" "Play with me, Grandma!" After all, the prospect of spending time with the grandchildren was the main reason for the visit! The children's parents are not likely to interfere, knowing that the children are the main attraction for us.

But if we do not want fatigue and its consequent irritability to lead to Hassles Number Four, Five, Six, and so on, we must be willing to say no now and then, and withdraw for a rest. A grown granddaughter recalled for me the visits to her grandmother's house years ago, and how grandmother insisted that the children take a nap every day after lunch, even though the girls were ten and twelve years old and long past the age for afternoon naps. Only now, when she is a grown woman with children of her own, has she realized that the enforced nap time was not for the children's sake. It was Grandma who needed that nap.

We may not need a nap. But we might do with a quiet hour alone in our own room, or a solitary stroll, or an errand undertaken by ourselves. Any excuse will do, just to get us out of the family hubbub and by ourselves for a bit. After the respite we can plunge in again, refreshed, and enjoy the fun without being distracted by the confusion.

When we are guests in their house it is not always easy to find a quiet spot. For this reason, some grandparents prefer to stay in a hotel or motel, even when there is room for them in the son's or daughter's house. And some grandparents, when having the young family visit them, take a room in the hotel and leave their house or apartment to the children. That way they at least get a good night's sleep.

Friends of mine borrowed the house of a friend nearby who happened to be going away at the convenient time. One grandmother borrowed an apartment in the same building, larger than her own, and offered it to the children. When the children declined—her apartment, however cramped, was more like home to them—she used her friend's apartment herself.

In Their House

When we are visiting in our son's or daughter's house we are guests, and we try to be good guests. We make our own bed and offer to make the others, take over some household chores, take the children out for an hour or an afternoon to relieve their mother. We go on errands, do some marketing, cook a meal or prepare a special dish.

A friend quoted me the axiom: In your daughter's house you're a help, in your daughter-in-law's a critic. That's an exaggeration, but it is true enough that your daughter-in-law is likely to be self-conscious when you visit. You try your best to put her at her ease. You appreciate her skills and ask for her recipes. You admire when admiration is due, and you never, never criticize. And you don't give advice unless asked, and then only in the spirit of a shared friendship, woman to woman. Never as a mother-in-law, telling her daughter-in-law how to cater to her son's comfort as she used to do. You are not so innocent as to fall into that stereotype. Nor do you instruct her in how to care for your grandchildren. Her ways of mothering may not be the same as yours were, but they are her children, not yours. You try your best to keep all that in mind.

Most important, you obey her house rules. One grandmother tells me that her daughter-in-law is glad to have her pitch in with dusting and vacuum cleaning. But setting and clearing the table, loading and unloading the dishwasher, are tasks that she has assigned to her ten- and eight-year-old daughters, and grandmother is not to relieve them. There are other tasks that are not specifically assigned, and grandmother can take a hand with the children in doing them.

Part of the pleasure of being with our grandchildren is doing things with them, useful tasks as well as play. A busy mother does not always have time to let the young children help her and learn while helping, and when they get older the children do not volunteer. But when grandmother is visiting, they come into her room to say good morning, and stay to help her make her bed and tidy up her room. And then she goes to their room and helps them make their beds, and perhaps she and they go on to make their parents' bed. And meanwhile she shows them how to make mitred corners when they tuck in the covers at the foot, and how to lay the top sheet wrong side up so that it folds back over the blanket to show the border right side out.

We were busy at this task in my daughter's house, when I was astonished to see my very young grandchildren struggling to tuck in the open ends of the pillow slip. "Where did you learn that?" I asked. "Mama does it," they said. I said to the older one, "Of course, I taught her that when she was a little girl like you." And when the younger one, who was three, shouted in sudden realization, "Our Mama was your little girl!" we all three laughed and hugged each other in delighted affirmation of a wonderful fact that was not really news to any of us.

For me the delight went deeper. One would hardly expect the trick of tucking in the ends of a pillow slip to become a symbol of tradition, handed on from generation to generation. But there it was, a housewifely habit that my mother had long ago taught to me, and I had taught to my daughter, becoming immortal in the small hands of my grandchildren. A visit with them in their own house can turn up all sorts of minute but memorable moments like this.

Then there are the bedtimes. Grandparents, especially grandfathers, are star performers at bedtime storytelling and tucking in. But again, we remember the house rules, and if bedtime is at a certain hour we are careful not to overstep the time, however reluctant we are to say goodnight to the children.

And mealtimes. At meals we do not mention eating the vegetables, or finishing what is on one's plate before one gets dessert, or minding one's table manners. I have never understood why any grandmother ever wanted to arrogate to herself such parental burdens, when it is our prime privilege as grandmothers to take no responsibility whatever for discipline.

With an Eye to Comfort

But there is one responsibility we must be willing to take, and that is for our own comfort. Our children's homes—whether city apartments, suburban split-levels, or country makeovers—are rarely spacious, not to say luxurious. In many cases they are of the make-do style of furnishing—have we forgotten our own early board-and-brick bookcases and hand-me-down sofas? Even when they have the look of conventional comfort, the spare room to which we are conducted usually doubles as the study, the den—by any other name, it is the little room with the desk where bills are paid, checkbooks balanced, and the painful economics of household management are worked out. Or else it is the living room, where the sofa, in a hospitable family like our children's, is a convertible.

Well and good. But one grandmother of my acquaintance, an avid bedtime reader, always carries her own small, collapsible Tensor lamp, which clamps to any convenient shelf or table edge. The same with clocks. One grandmother purloins the children's electric alarm clock and undertakes to get them up for school during her visit—she enjoys preparing and eating breakfast with them. And another grandmother simply brings her own traveling clock and knows what time it is without help from the local facilities.

As for drawer space and closet space, we are also often very much on our own. The study guest room has no dresser drawers, nor has the living room, and neither room has a clothes closet. We may settle for living out of a suitcase, and find hangers in the outdoor coat closet for whatever wardrobe we bring.

Some grandmothers have noticed a curious phenomenon: Sons-in-law and daughters-in-law treat us as guests, and they go out of their way to make us feel welcome. A son-in-law rarely forgets to help his mother-in-law out of the car, carry her bags upstairs, open the window in the guest room that always sticks. A daughter-in-law puts out her best bedspread and nicest towels for us, has plenty of hangers in the closet and a bowl of fresh flowers on the dresser. If the guest room is the study or the living room, she will somehow contrive to give us a drawer for our underthings and closet space for our clothes.

But our daughters and sons, however devoted and thoughtful of us in the more important concerns of life, seem somehow to take it for granted that mother will manage for herself. Grandmothers have talked with me about this puzzling behavior in their otherwise considerate children. And the conclusions they have arrived at have struck me as entirely convincing and—in a way—touching.

Our in-law children know us as we are now, mature women of a certain age who might like their comforts attended to. But our own sons and daughters still see us as the capable young mothers we were in their childhood. In their eyes we do not grow old. It does not occur to them that in our fifties or more we are not about to camp out in a sleeping bag on the floor as we may have done in our young motherhood days, or tote bulging shopping bags and suitcases as we used to do with the greatest of ease when we traveled about with them as children.

So their apparent unconcern for our comfort is only a leftover of old parent-child patterns. We may never have been the kind of mothers who asked a child to run upstairs and fetch this, fetch that, see where we have left something or other. If mother usually did these things for herself during their growing-up years, then that is how they still think of her today. They would never fail her if something important were involved. But a need for small attentions doesn't go with their picture of mother.

And so grandmothers who are old hands at visiting do not find their grown son's or daughter's oversights a cause for hurt feelings. On the contrary, they are rather amused, even flattered. For my own part—call me sentimental if you like—I find it, as I have said, rather touching that in our children's eyes we are forever young.

That does not mean we have to live up to it. We don't like to be thought of as fussy old women, but neither do we have to play along with the illusion of youth, however charming, and pretend that we enjoy roughing it. Without shattering our children's image of us, we can nevertheless make our wants known. Or we can do as we have done in the past—we can attend to them ourselves.

One grandmother who finds her daughter's sofa uncomfortably hard and narrow simply orders in a rented collapsible bed for the duration of her stay. Another one made a present to her daughter-in-law of a roll-away bed, after first consulting with her about whether there was space to store it. Another makes no bones about asking her daughter for the extra blanket and pillow from the top of the storage closet, and still another brings her own small, firm pillow, which she prefers to her daughter-in-law's large soft ones. There is always a way to compromise between the comfort we make for ourselves at home and downright discomfort when we visit, and it is up to ourselves to find a tactful, uncritical way to achieve it.

In Our House

When our young families are coming to visit us, we generally turn ourselves and our homes inside out to prepare for them. Some of us shop and cook and bake right up to the minute they are due to arrive. We can hardly stop thinking of something else to do, something more to prepare, that will please them. And that's our first mistake, because by the time they come we are already tired out—when the one thing we know we will need is our strength. How much wiser to leave the last little things undone—they will never be missed—and lie down with our feet up until they come, or until it is time to go and meet them.

For a son or daughter, coming home to mother's is like going backward in time to their childhood. And while recapturing their youth may mean all kinds of nostalgic pleasures, it can also mean reviving some of the not-so-nice habits. Your daughter as well as your granddaughter kicks her shoes off in the living room and forgets them there. Your son as well as your grandson shucks off a coat, a sweater, a scarf, wherever he happens to be, leaves his suitcase in the hall where he used to leave his skates for you to trip over, drops a paper wrapping here, abandons a glass there (and leaves a ring on the table top)—it is the same mixture as before.

When they were children in your house you kept after them to pick things up. But now they are guests, and you don't want to spoil their visit with scolding. So you patiently go around the house picking up after your grown children as well as your grandchildren.

Said one grandmother, "It's bad enough to have to walk over the tinker-toys to serve dinner. But when it comes to wading through the Sunday papers! . . ." Still, we do it, and with hardly a murmur. It is wonderful what a grandmother will put up with.

Why do we? Do we need to? Are we afraid they will love us less if we protest? We obey their house rules when we visit them. What about our house rules?

When they were children we used to give them a five-minute warning to pick up their things before dinner and bedtime. What is wrong with enforcing the same rules now that they are grown? It is no bad thing for the grandchildren, too, to learn that grandmother's house has its rules, however gently imposed.

The eight-, nine-, ten-year-olds, accustomed to tearing around in their own house, can surely be asked to go more quietly in grandmother's house. If it is a city apartment, there are neighbors downstairs and next door. If it is grandmother's house standing by itself, there is still grandmother's desire for quietness. The teen-age grandchildren can be asked to turn the hi-fi or the TV down to more reasonable decibels, not only for the neighbors but for grandmother's comfort as well.

We need not be tyrannical about these matters, but neither need we feel apologetic when we try to keep a little of the orderliness and serenity of our houses during their visits. Children accept it, and they accommodate to it. They also know how to be good guests, even if we have to remind them now and then.

What is more, they like it. They look to grandmother's house to be different from their own. They expect it to be different. They recognize the relative tidiness, the nice things that they must be careful of (but best put away the fragile old things and the porcelains). They understand that grandmother's house is not a place in which you run and jump and fling yourself and your things around. You do not play ball in Grandma's living room (if indeed you do in your mother's, which one doubts). You do not pick leaves off Grandma's house plants. You do not leave your toy car on Grandma's stairs.

We more than make up for these restraints with the unexpected pleasures we can give them. Your granddaughter discovers that you still use the funny, lopsided bowl she made for you in kindergarten. Your grandson comes upon the ill-fitted, lumpily painted box he made for you with his first tool set, or the smudgily decorated bookmark, still keeping your place in your bedside reading. "Grandma, that's the bookmark I made!" they positively crow with the joy of recognition. Grandma doesn't tell them how often she has been tempted to clear them out, or at least to put them in a box on a top shelf, and then has kept them in sight after all, the way she keeps their pictures where she can see them day after day.

Most of us manage to keep something old. In one grandmother's house the children's favorite over the years was an antique high chair, plain and sturdy, lovingly made by some early American country craftsman, its little seat and arms so polished by the years that they felt almost soft to the touch. It had been a present to her first child, and after her son and daughter were grown and married it had been sat in by each of the grandchildren in turn. Finally came a visit when her youngest grandchild was sitting in it. She was seven, but small and neatly made, and as she eased into the tiny seat she said rather sadly, "Grandma, I think this is the last time I'll be able to fit into the high chair."

Another grandmother still has what were the double-decker bunk beds from her children's room, which she now uses as twin beds in her guest room. Before the family came to visit, she had a man come in and put them together as a double-decker again, in order to make space in the room for a third bed. And no sooner had the family arrived than the expected argument broke out among the grandchildren. Who was going to have the choice sleeping place, the upper bunk? And in the timeless manner of children, the argument ended in drawing lots and taking turns, and one of them at once sat down to make a chart of whose turn it would be each night.

While all this was going on, grandmother, a careful saver, went up to the attic and brought down the original chart, drawn and decorated with crayons, that the children's mother had made when she and her brother, their uncle, had also battled over who was to have the upper berth. The children's delight in this was past measuring, and it is still one of their favorite stories when they play the family game of "Remember that time when?"

We often feel that our children's and our grandchildren's lives have moved so very far from our own, their world so changed, their concerns so different. We need discoveries like these to reassure us that things haven't changed altogether. There is a continuity, an immutable bond—and we are the link. It is a reassurance not only to us, but to our children and perhaps even more to our grandchildren. They need these ties to the past no less than we need them, and it is when they come to visit at our house that we rediscover and relive them together.

Babysitting

Whatever else we may do, babysitting seems to be the most typically grandmotherly service that is expected of us, and one that most of us seem to enjoy. It gives us the children without the parents, and that's a universal grandmotherly desire fulfilled. It gives us a responsibility and a feeling of being needed. But if we live nearby and are often called upon, however much we love our grandchildren it can become a burden.

When grandmother feels put upon with too much babysitting, she has her choices. She can make whatever excuse comes readily to mind. She can offer to pay a babysitter in her stead. Or she can simply decline—no, dear, not this time. If the children's parents do not get the message, it is always possible to tell them that there are limits to one's time and energy. I do not hold with grandmothers allowing themselves to be exploited.

When we live nearby we may have the choice of babysitting in the grandchildren's house or our own. One grandmother tells me she prefers her own, especially during the daytime, because in her own house she has better control of lively, active children. Babies and toddlers can be kept in or taken out, but school-age children can hardly be locked in the house. They want to be out with their playmates.

We cannot always keep track of where they are, and we are likely to have some uneasy hours. When they are in our house we may make our own rules about going out to play. At the same time, if we take them away from their normal haunts and playmates, then in all fairness we ought to have some other arrangements for their entertainment.

When we are in charge in their house, whatever their parents' rules, we are free to add our own. Play time, nap time, bedtime—we are not obliged to follow slavishly a routine that wears us out. "Mommy lets us!" the children protest. Perhaps Mommy does, but Mommy is not Grandma, and her energies may be more elastic than grandmother's, or her nerves more sturdy.

Walking a mountain trail with my youngsters one day, I was horrified to discover them waving to me from high up on a sheer rock face. How did they get there? "Oh, there's a path, Grandma—see, right back there!" Grandma saw, and quailed. I am a walker but no mountain goat, and I could not follow them. On the other hand, I could not let them go unaccompanied. So I called to them to come down. "Daddy lets us!" they called back. "It's okay, we're careful!" What is Grandma to do? This grandmother was in no doubt. I ordered them down. But I did feel that I had to apologize. I did not doubt that they were careful, but I could not let them go where I was unable to follow.

The children are nice enough about accommodating to grandmother's city muscles and her grandmotherly nerves. Still, we don't like to restrict their enjoyment too much, or they will feel that when Grandma is in charge it's no fun. So when we deprive them of one kind of fun we are in honor bound to provide them with another, of a kind that they can have only with grandmother. What that may be is up to each of us. Every grandmother has, or develops, her own bag of tricks.

When they go out to play, we want to know where they will be and with whom. When they go to a friend's house, we are well within our rights in accompanying them there, to see where they will be and what they will be doing, and especially whether a mother or some other adult is in charge. We are also within our rights in setting a time for their return. If grandmother seems to fuss too much, she can always explain that she doesn't know their neighborhood and their friends the way Mommy does, and she would like to become acquainted. If letting them out of her sight for too long still makes her anxious, she can always make the counter-suggestion that the friend come to their house instead.

For a grandmother who lives far away, it is a particular pleasure to babysit in the children's house, to see and participate in their daily life and their daily routine. I have liked walking to school with my school-age granddaughter, letting her show me her classroom and introduce me to her teacher. I have liked going to the day-care center with my grandson, who calls it his school. I have been reassured by chatting with the people who look after him while his mother is at work, and watching him at play with the other working mothers' children there.

These are ways that make a grandmother, especially an absentee grandmother, part of her grandchildren's lives. We used to visit our children's schools when we were mothers, talk to their teachers, go to the parent-teacher meetings. We are a step removed from that, as grandmothers, but one of the ways in which we may enjoy our grandchildren—and in some situations, allay our anxieties about them—is in having this actual day-to-day glimpse of their lives in their own homes. It is not every grandmother's way, but I have found it rewarding.

Anxiety is an inevitable part of babysitting, and we deal with it as we may. One prohibition we must really observe.

The anxiety is strictly our own, not to be displayed to the children. Our task is to make our babysitting visit as ordinary as we can, with whatever grandmotherly trimmings we care to add in the form of fun and games. We are the bearers of stability and serenity. When we lose our cool, we are muffing the job.

The Grandmother House

The first time I heard of a grandmother house was when a dear friend, a woman past retirement age but still working at her profession, bought a delightful little house in the country. It was well beyond commuting from her city job and her city apartment, but she did not have to explain why she had bought it. She had grandchildren growing up in distant parts, and this was where she hoped they might come from time to time to spend vacations with her.

Then I heard of another and another, in the Vermont woods, on a seagirt island off the Massachusetts coast, on the Pacific coast. That was when I began to call them grandmother houses.

Many people who can afford it buy a second home in a pleasant place—in the ski country, near the lake or seashore. They talk about it as a vacation home and eventually as a retirement home. They do not always think of it as a grandmother house. But some do, and more might well do so.

Now that the family homestead is a thing of the past, and so many parents give up the big old house and move to a manageable apartment when the children grow up and establish their own homes, we need a modern version of the house for the children to come home to. That's the grandmother house.

A California couple, planning their retirement home, thought first of making it a place for their grandchildren to visit. They built a small, easily maintained house for themselves, and then they added a guest house. When the grandchildren come, the guest house and the surrounding land are theirs. The grandparents helped the children build a tree house, and there are always ongoing projects around the place to which the children return on their visits. The grandparents' retirement is enhanced by the life and activity of the grandchildren around them—and the grandchildren have the loving companionship of their grandparents to look forward to on their vacations.

A couple I know in a middlewestern city did it the other way round. When all but the youngest of their children had left home, instead of moving to a smaller house or an apartment they bought a big, rambling, grandmotherish house in an old residential neighborhood in town. They did not yet have a grandchild, but they had married children. Their friends saw it as rather funny, because through all the years while their children were growing up they had stayed on in the old house which, although pleasant, was rather a tight fit for the family. Their friends reminded them, too, that as each child grew up and married, this mother used to say, "Fine, another one launched," and "Babysit? Not for me. I'm glad to have finished my job." Now, she says, since they have been thrifty all those years, they can afford the luxury of an anticipatory grandmother house.

I haven't heard of any others doing it this way, and most people looking forward to grandparenthood wouldn't consider a house except in the country or at the shore. But for young grandparents whose retirement is still years in the future, a comfortable old house in town, with trees and a garden and a big back yard, is not all that impractical as a place to live and to have the children and grandchildren visit. To me, at any rate, it has the charm of deliberately turning the clock back to a more tranquil era when American families still lived in such houses. Besides, we expect young parents to move into bigger houses in anticipation of coming children. Why shouldn't young grandparents do the same in anticipation of coming grandchildren?

Our needs do not change—the satisfaction of them only comes around again in a new form. The grandmother house is a new answer to an old longing, the longing to have our children and grandchildren around us. Perhaps not all the time, but now and then.

A Poem

Grandmother was in the parlor already: bending and leaning over the arm of a chair, she was standing at the wall and praying fervently. Papa stood near her. She turned around to us and smiled, when she noticed that we were hiding behind our backs the presents which we were to offer. . . .

"Well, do show us, Nikolenka! What is it you have, a box or a drawing?" said papa to me. There was nothing to be done; with a trembling hand I gave her the crushed, fatal roll; but my voice refused to serve me, and I stopped silent before grandmother. I was beside myself, thinking that, instead of the expected drawing, they would read aloud my worthless poem. How am I to tell the agony through which I passed, when grandmother began to read aloud my poem; when, unable to make it out, she stopped in the middle of the verse in order to look at papa with a smile, which then seemed to me to be one of mockery; and when, her eyes being weak, she did not finish reading it, but handed it to papa and asked him to read it from the beginning? It seemed to me that she did so because she was tired of reading such horrible and badly scrawled verses. . . . I was waiting for him to snap my nose with the poem. . . . But nothing of the sort happened; on the contrary, after it had been read, grandmother said: "*Charmant!*" and kissed my brow.

—*Childhood*, from *Complete Works of Count Tolstoy*

6

One at a Time

Whether they live near or far away, there is one device that every experienced grandmother knows when it comes to weaving bonds with the grandchildren.

In one grandmother's blunt words: Get rid of the parents.

Another went into detail. Family visits are all very well, but they do not half do the job, she said. When the family is all there together, not only the children but the parents compete. They are all siblings. And the parents put the grandchildren on parade. "Say hello to Grandma. . . ." "Give Grandma a kiss. . . ." "Say thank you to Grandma. . . ." "Give Grandma that comfortable chair. . . ." If the visit is in grandmother's house, the cautions are a running stream—"Don't touch . . . don't be so noisy . . . you're getting sticky fingers all over Grandma's nice sofa . . . of course you're going to eat that nice supper Grandma cooked for you. . . ." If the children love us in spite of all this they are haloed saints.

Grandmothers go to great lengths, even push the parents out of their own house, to get the children alone. Taking them one at a time is the next step.

Some parents are acute enough to do this with their own children, with whom it is after all not easy. It means making special arrangements for an hour or an afternoon alone with one child. Grandmothers only need to issue an invitation, or seize an opportunity when one presents itself.

When we are spending a longish visit with the young family, in their house or ours, the opportunities to capture a grandchild alone are bound to occur. On a summer vacation together they may go swimming in a herd, but there are quiet times when one wants to read with us, and another will pick berries, go rock hunting, shell collecting, exploring in the woods or fields. One loves to go marketing and another considers it a great treat to go along to the garbage dump.

The memorable times, for them as for us, are the visits to grandmother's house alone. Only then do we discover each other, not as stereotyped grandmother and grandchild, but as people. And all we have to do is invite them to visit us, one at a time.

All we have to do? Grandmother can be forgiven if she suffers a spot of stage fright. Yet it is no big deal, especially if they live nearby. We make a date for a Saturday, a Sunday, a weekend if the child would like that. Some grandparents make the child's birthday the occasion for a special festive visit, no matter how many unbirthday visits there may also be in the course of the year. The birthday visit alone with grandparents is different from the family birthday party with the child's friends. It can include a surprise treat of something we know—or guess—the child would like to see or do, as well as the birthday cake complete with candles and presents.

Going Places, Doing Things

Birthday or unbirthday, when we have a grandchild to ourselves we plan to do something together that suits both the child's taste and our own—unless a common interest has not yet developed, in which case we follow the child's lead and do something he or she wants to do. Failing that, we take a chance.

We may be within reach of some specific children's entertainment, a puppet show, a special movie, sometimes a play for young audiences. A grandmother looking for a treat for her grandchild can easily find out what is going on.

I am a little wary of some children's entertainment—even Disney witches have given some youngsters nightmares. I remember a fine stage performance of a fairy tale to which I took a young nephew years ago. It had a scene in which the wicked witch turned the child hero into a pie, and the magic was stage-managed so effectively that half a dozen small viewers screamed in terror and had to be taken hastily out of the theater. Perhaps their present-day diet of television horrors prepares them somewhat better for such surprises, but we must remember that a live performance or a life-size movie still has more reality than the little illuminated screen.

A granddaughter fond of clothes can be taken shopping at any age, and so, I find, can a grandson if he is young enough. A child of either sex can enjoy a science or industry show, a visit to the zoo, the natural history museum or one of the new science museums, or the art museum. Museums are a ball these days. They have taken not merely a leaf but a whole book from the entertainment business, and have made some of their displays so entertaining that if we haven't paid them a visit in the past few years we are due for some agreeable surprises. There are usually special exhibits for children of various ages, and some museums have whole sections for young visitors. Or am I telling you something you don't need to be told? So many grandmothers are not only dedicated museum goers but members and supporters of their museums.

The child's young age is not necessarily a measure of his potential interests—I am thinking of our four-year-old's passion for dinosaurs. But we are wise to watch for signs of flagging attention, and we need to know our own fatigue thresholds. Best to make a first museum trip a fairly brief one, and not to cover too much ground. It goes without saying that if we inform ourselves beforehand about something special to see, the visit is likely to be the more successful.

Hours at home can be happily spent working together over jigsaw puzzles, model planes, boats, toy furniture, a doll house, or cutting out and dressing paper dolls. A grandmother needlewoman can help cut out and sew doll clothes. She can spend a marvelous day with a young teen-ager who wants to learn to sew, shopping for a pattern and dress material, and another day laying out the pattern, cutting out the skirt or blouse or whatever, basting and fitting and sewing. And still another day, perhaps, finishing, with all the nice details with which a good dressmaker puts her mark on the work.

But if learning is to be a pleasure, grandmother cannot be too severe a taskmaster. One grandmother told me how she had been rebuked by her older granddaughter for being too much of a perfectionist with the younger one. The younger girl, who was twelve and already very good with her hands, had been so enthusiastic after her first sewing lesson with Grandma that she had gone ahead and finished the dress by herself, staying up half the night to do so. Grandma praised her, but apparently not enough, because she had gone on to show the child where she had done this and that wrong, and had ended by saying they would rip it all out together on Saturday and do it again properly. The twelve-year-old was silent and downcast—and so was grandmother, who realized that she perhaps had discouraged forever what might have developed into a fine skill. And so she might. But that particular story had a happy ending, for the child arrived on Saturday with all her work carefully ripped apart, ready to begin again and learn how to do it the right way.

Is This Wasteful?

Then there is cooking, or more often baking. An afternoon spent making a batch of cookies, gingerbread men, a birthday cake for mother, father, or a sibling—or even learning to bake bread—why not? Five-year-olds, both boys and girls, do it in the progressive kindergartens. What if milk spills and eggs splatter?

I once talked about this with the principal of my children's school, the late Caroline Pratt who was one of the great pioneers in the education of young children. She told me with some indignation that there were parents who had expressed their disapproval at what they called the wastefulness of letting young children work with the actual ingredients of puddings and cookies and bread. So much of it goes on their faces, their clothes, the floor! And she said, "Imagine, considering educational materials a waste! We should be concerned about wasting our children's eagerness to learn, rather than about wasting some flour and a few eggs!"

I have never forgotten that, and I pass it on to you. If we have not thought about flour and eggs—or dress materials and knitting yarns—as educational materials when we were mothers, as grandmothers we can surely afford to.

And so we tie on the big aprons and get to work. If they make mistakes and have accidents, if things slip and spill and our immaculate kitchen looks like the combined effects of flood and cyclone when it is over, never mind. What we value as grandmothers is the child. What is a clean kitchen worth, compared with the joy of a child who has actually produced a miniature loaf of bread with his or her own hands? We may have to overcome the habits of a lifetime, and bite our tongues rather than give utterance to the automatic cautions (Look out! That's spilling! Watch what you're doing now!) but it is worth it all if at the end the child has something to show for it.

As for the mess, part of the shared experience is the cleaning up together afterward. And let's not be too fussy about that either. We can always go back and put things to rights after the visit is over.

Boy and Girl Stuff

Boys will joyfully take part in these culinary sessions (don't Daddies cook nowadays?) at least when they are little. At nine, ten, eleven, they may be keener about other experiences—and so may girls. Grandmother's afternoon may be spent doing what *they* want to do, and that may mean the Little League baseball game or perhaps a pair of seats for the big league game.

A friend in Houston, Texas, told me of complimenting a grandmother on her nice grandchildren, who always took her along to the baseball and football games. "Thank you," said grandmother, "they *are* nice children, but not because they take me to the games. You see, they're my tickets!"

That grandmother has season tickets to the Astrodome every year for her grandchildren, and she always goes along. What matter if Grandma cheers at the wrong moments, as one grandson wryly told us in that little book of children's comments? Not all that many of us grew up with baseball, football, soccer, ice hockey (to be sure, at a recent game of the New York Mets one of the fans was celebrating her 101st birthday) but we can learn. The excitement and good humor of an American sports crowd is infectious all by itself, and there is the spectacle besides, to say nothing of the hot dogs and pop, the peanuts, the ice cream. For a really committed grandmother, even if these delights may pall, an afternoon of sharing a grandchild's enthusiasm is pleasure enough, whether or not she understands the game.

When Grandmother Leads

With all that we have said, grandmother still has her options. None of this, not the museum or the cooking or the ball game, may appeal to her, and she does not have to do any of it. She need not follow the child's lead, certainly not exclusively. One of the finest things she can do for a grandchild is to give the child a bit of herself—to share one of her own interests.

Whatever it is—handicrafts, gardening, painting, bird watching, butterflies, even a passion for rare books—it can be shared with a child. Not with every child, but then the whole point of taking the grandchildren one at a time is to discover what we can share with each.

A grown granddaughter recalled affectionately for me how her grandmother, who loved words, used to play rhyming games with her, and taught her how to use the dictionary. This same young woman was also fortunate in her grandfather, a horticulturist, with whom as a child she spent hours working in his greenhouse, incidentally learning to call the plants by their names and how to grow and care for them. These are gifts from her grandparents that she has treasured, and no doubt will treasure all her life.

Of course when grandmother takes the lead she may get the bit in her teeth and run away, dragging the weary child behind her. One grandmother took her grandchild on an afternoon tour of all the flea markets and antique shops in her country neighborhood, and there were many. The seven-year-old granddaughter enjoyed the first two or three, but by the fifth she asked to stay in the car, and after that she spent the rest of the day curled up in her seat, either fast asleep or pretending to be.

That grandmother's particular passion was old tinware, or maybe it was buttons, I forget. Now if it had been antique dolls, the little girl's attention might have lasted a bit longer. But even with an enthusiasm that the child can share, there are limits to how far we can impose our own obsession on a guest, especially a young one who cannot protest and has no escape.

We need to give thought to what aspect of our enthusiasm might strike a spark with a child. A single visit to a fine collection of antique dolls and doll houses and doll furniture might have made a memorable afternoon for that little girl, especially if it ended with a sit-down treat of ice cream and cookies. Or a trip to see one of those reconstructed colonial rooms in the museum, with the home-made baby's cradle, the child-size rocker, the pots and kettles in the fireplace, the crude dishes and tableware, the spinning wheel and the utensils and the tools.

If you think rare books must be an impossible reach for a child, there are collections in some libraries—perhaps in your own town—of children's books of past centuries. A child of our time can have hilarious fun over those moralistic illustrations of naughty children and their horrendous punishments. I see that one of the fiercest children's books of the past, the notorious *Struwwel-Peter*, is reprinted for children today. I can only hope it is meant as a joke.

Would you believe archeology might be something to share with a grandchild? A woman who always loved to travel discovered after her children had grown up that ruins had a fascination for her, and from ruins she went on to visit archeological digs. When she became a grandmother she began sending postcards to her grandchildren from all the exotic sites she visited, and she found that the children saved the cards.

Now, as each of her four grandchildren reaches the age of twelve, she takes them one by one on a trip of her choice. She is the kind of knowing traveler who does her homework for a trip beforehand, and she shares the preparation and the planning with the lucky child whose turn it is to go. As a souvenir of the trip after it is over, she and the child decorate a large map with stamps they have collected from the region, and they mark each spot where they have been in color on the map.

The first grandchild who went set another precedent. He gave a talk for his classmates in school, illustrated with postcards and photographs and, of course, the map. He invited grandmother as his co-speaker, but in proper grandmotherly style she left the lecture and demonstration to him and contributed a fact or a comment only when she was asked.

Even a small excursion—to another city, another state—can be interesting to a child. I know a grandmother who ordinarily goes no farther than she can walk. She is an ardent walker, and although in our automobile age it is not easy to find times and places for walking she manages to do so. But she is aware that this, to her, highly rewarding pleasure has little appeal to children all by itself—few children will walk for walking's sake. So she has exerted her imagination to make an hour's or an afternoon's walk interesting to a child.

It becomes an exploration—if in the city, to an interesting neighborhood or an old one, or the riverfront or the harbor. If in the country, it can be an excursion to a woodland, a pond, a stream, or a walk along a beach to collect shells and stones. Children can become interested in ways of identifying trees, birds, butterflies, bugs, all as part of a walk. This woman had a whole New England village of children walking with her one summer, gathering specimens of wildflowers and later of their berries, to identify together in her wildflower books. It was good training for grandmotherhood, she says. She now has her grandchildren walking with her, sharing her interests in the same way that the village children shared them.

Another woman started one of her grandsons stargazing. They had a week together at the seashore once at the end of summer, when all the summer people had left and his school term had not yet begun, and the boy had nothing much to do and no one his own age to do it with. So they began to go down to the beach after supper, with a flashlight and a map of the heavens, and on those cold brilliant September nights they explored the sky together. For the boy it was the beginning of a lifelong amateur interest in astronomy. Another boy learned weather-watching—from a grandfather, who was an amateur meteorologist—and for him it was the beginning of a meteorological career.

We never know in advance how precious a gift we may be giving a grandchild when we share something of ourselves with him or her alone. A skill, an interest, an enthusiasm that we lovingly lay open to a child may add life and color to that child's entire life to come. When we think of our own lives, we discover that some of our own dearest interests were born in us during childhood, and often its first discovery came with the help of a beloved adult, a parent, grandparent, uncle, aunt, a grown cousin, a family friend. The work many people must do for a living is rarely gratifying in itself, and the way the world is going our grandchildren are even more likely than we or their parents have been to be pushing buttons and feeding computers. What finer bequest can we give them than an interest that will absorb and enrich their leisure?

A wise physician I once knew said that most people would

live healthier and happier lives if they did not put their childhood toys in the attic, but kept them to play with through the years. Those lifelong toys are what we give our grandchildren when we share our dearest interests with them.

The Unplanned Visit

Sometimes an opportunity to have a grandchild alone presents itself unsought. In one family the younger grandchildren, two little girls, had quite naturally made themselves at home in grandmother's house, but the eldest, a boy, had drawn away to his own interests in the middle school years and the grandmother felt she scarcely knew him. Then one summer, just before he was to go to summer camp, he broke his arm. The family was to go away two weeks later, but here were two weeks when the boy's friends were all away and he would have nothing to do. Seeing him disappointed and disconsolate, grandmother asked if he would like to visit her and his grandfather at their cottage in the country.

Those two weeks were memorable for all three. The grandparents discovered their grandson and the grandson discovered his grandparents. There were other boys his age in the neighborhood, but although he was friendly he did not seek their company. He preferred to work beside grandmother—one-armed, to be sure—in the garden, or with grandfather who was repairing the porch. He shared their early morning and twilight strolls. They had known him as rather a silent boy when the whole family was together, but after the first uneasy day of being alone with them he began opening up, and for two weeks they never had a moment's pause in finding something to talk about together.

Another unplanned visit was the arrival of a runaway grandson. This was an only child who was going through a rough period in his adolescence, and he had withdrawn into himself, away from his friends, away from his understanding and loving parents. He had been cutting school and had fallen behind, as often happens in these difficult years, and he had come to hate the public high school where he was in his second year.

And so one morning, instead of going to school, he boarded a bus. He rode aimlessly all day, taking one bus after another, and by late evening he found himself, perhaps by unconscious design, in a town a few miles from his grandparents' house. He got off the bus, hoofed the distance, and arrived at their door tired, dirty, hungry, and with not a word to say for himself.

His grandparents knew he had been unhappy, and they had known for several hours that he had not come home from school. A quick reassuring phone call to his parents, and then grandmother without fussing got the boy fed, showered, and to bed. The next day the parents arrived, and the boy made it clear that he would not go back to his school, didn't care if he never went back to school, didn't want to go home to the city. The only proposal he said yes to was that he would stay with his grandparents if they would have him. His parents agreed to let him stay in this safe refuge, no matter if he lost the year at school.

He stayed through the winter and all that spring. He shoveled the path after snowstorms for his grandfather, helped plant the garden, carried grandmother's groceries from the car, made himself generally useful. But he still did not talk about what was troubling him. Nor did he ever. He simply worked things out within himself. When the time came for a decision about the next school year, he said he would like to go to a country school. So a boarding school was chosen, and the unhappy runaway, after his odd and hermitlike retreat in his grandparents' house, went cheerfully off to his new school where he distinguished himself as a student and a fine school athlete.

A dramatic story, and surely not a usual one, but it illustrates a point. There may come a time in any child's life when he or she is fed up with family, siblings, school, or whatever. Usually it is an unselective grab bag of discontents, and it is a time when a child needs a refuge, a surcease from the everyday irritants, a holiday, long or short, in which to sort things out. And that's a time when grandmother's house may be the place to run away to.

The child may not have any thought of running away (although something like a million American children run away from home every year). But when grandmother hears and sees that one of the grandchildren is not getting along in the family, she can surely make a suggestion to the parents, and with their permission she can invite the child to visit her for a night, a weekend, or longer.

If it is to be for any substantial period, she would be wise to think about what she is undertaking. This is when it is especially important to know the child, to have a relationship with the child already established.

And I think it is important for grandmother to be clear in her own mind that she is not undertaking any sort of therapy for what is troubling the child. She is not going to examine and diagnose a case and then carry out treatment. All she is doing is giving this particular grandchild a holiday from home and family, and from school as well if that is indicated.

If the child wants to talk, there are loving grandparents to listen. If not, there is a safe and peaceful refuge in which to work things out. We can—indeed we should—establish house rules, which the child must agree to keep while under our roof. The rules will of course be tailored to the child's age, but if we are to take responsibility for him he must be responsible in his behavior to us. Comings and goings, mealtimes, bedtimes, a degree of order in his room and his possessions—all that is reasonable to ask, and oddly enough, whatever their unruliness at home, most boys and girls will keep to grandmother's house rules in grandmother's house. The consequences of not keeping them are implicit—if the child is not a good guest he will be sent home.

The rules for grandparents in such a situation are not to hover, not to pry, not to surround the child with a cloud of anxiety. That is part of what he is escaping from. What he needs at such times, and what his parents are not able to give him mainly because they are his parents, is a matter-of-fact acceptance that he is dealing with his problems and a confidence that he will resolve them in due time.

As grandmothers we have had enough experience of life to know that, given a little time, most children do work things out. They do come out of their tunnel, if we have the patience to wait, and unobtrusively to watch. If the child's behavior seems to suggest more serious problems than he can handle by himself, we can always consult with his parents and suggest professional help.

Also as grandmothers, we are that one step farther removed from the child than his parents. We have the advantage of loving concern combined with objectivity that can be a most valuable support to a distressed child.

The Center of Our Household

My paternal grandmother, who lived with us from the time my parents married until she died in 1927, while I was studying anthropological collections in German museums, was the most decisive influence in my life. She sat at the center of our household. Her room—and my mother always saw to it that she had the best room, spacious and sunny, with a fireplace if possible—was the place to which we immediately went when we came in from playing or home from school. There my father went when he arrived in the house. There we did our lessons on the cherry-wood table with which she had begun housekeeping and which, later, was my dining room table for twenty-five years. There, sitting by the fire, erect and intense, she listened to us and to all of Mother's friends and to our friends. In my early childhood she was also very active—cooking, preserving, growing flowers in the garden, and attentive to all the activities of the country and the farm, including the chickens that were always invading the lawn and that I was always being called from my book to shoo away.

—*Blackberry Winter: My Earlier Years*,
by Margaret Mead

7

Under One Roof

A grandmother who lives under the same roof with her grandchildren should have no engineering problems when it comes to building bridges between herself and them. A long, rich history stands behind the three-generation household, establishing her status and defining her role in the family. The bridges linking her to the third generation are all in place, firmly supported by tradition.

Or so one would assume. But in our time many seemingly unshakable traditions have fallen to rubble. The three-generation family under one roof has not yet collapsed entirely, but it is tottering. The number of families that have a third adult, most often a grandparent, living with them has diminished sharply in the past decade or two.

Bare statistics do not communicate the impact of this change. A distinguished social scientist, Dr. Urie Bronfenbrenner of Cornell University, warns of the disastrous effect of the grandmotherless household on children. Commentators have described modern parents as abandoning their role in the nurturing of children, in the same way that they have been abandoning the grandparents.

So again we have a demonstration of the cynical aphorism that grandchildren and grandparents have the same enemy, the parents. When we examine that aphorism more closely we find it is not only cynical but simplistic. The parents, too, are victims of these cataclysmic social changes. Society gives them little or none of the help that they once had from the extended family in caring for either the young or the old who are dependent on them. In the nuclear family the double responsibility is that of the parents alone.

What wouldn't most working mothers give to have grandmother in the house as an instant—and dependable—solution to the never permanently solved problem of the children's day care? To say nothing of sharing the burdens of housekeeping, marketing, cooking, and giving the young parents some little freedom to enjoy their own social and recreational pleasures?

Provided, of course, that she is the right kind of grandmother. A University of North Carolina psychiatric team analyzed the early years of their child patients, and came up with the finding that many of these youngsters who had been left in grandmother's care suffered conflicts of love and loyalty, were torn between the contradictory demands made by mother and grandmother. And a Chicago psychoanalyst, Dr. Ernest A. Rappaport, has commented harshly on what he called the "grandparent syndrome" in the three-generation household. Too often, he observed, the grandparents take over the parental role and relegate the parents to the position of elder siblings. In some of these families the children actually call their mother Sis.

Grandfather escapes lightly in these strictures. He is a retired man, and in our world a man who is not earning is a man without power or authority. He becomes a rather passive, shadowy member of the household, if indeed he is there at all. Grandmother, alas, stands out as the chief menace to the children and their parents.

So perhaps we should look more closely at the aura of loving harmony that glows around our image of the vanishing three-generation family. It was not automatically ideal. Human individuality, human failings and follies cast their dark shadows even on that cherished tradition.

When it worked, it worked superbly. I think of Margaret Mead's grandmother, whom Dr. Mead recalled with gratitude when she herself became a grandmother. The elder Mrs. Mead moved into her son's house and shared the care of the children while her daughter-in-law studied for a graduate degree, and between them this pair of pioneer feminists created a sparkling household in which the five Mead children grew up. Grandmother Mead, a retired teacher well versed in experimental methods, was Dr. Mead's first teacher, and she remembers well her grandmother's methods of instilling in her the discipline of firsthand observation and recording that stood her in such good stead as a novice anthropologist in Samoa.

We must go back perhaps a century or more to see the American grandmother in her traditional role. That was when the single roof under which the generations lived together was the family homestead, and grandmother was the mistress in her own house. Once she gave up her house and came to live in her son's or daughter's house, she lost the essential framework that gave shape and meaning to her life. She became, like her retired husband, a displaced person, without power or place except as she could create them for herself.

Few people can survive such a displacement in their middle years without some loss of equilibrium. People who find themselves afloat, without root or anchor in their environment, tend to go to extremes. Either they assert a power that is not generically theirs—and we have heard the critics of these grandmothers who become not merely surrogate mothers to their grandchildren but mothers to the whole household, parents as well as children. Or they become humble shadows, shrinking from what they feel is an intrusion on the life of the nuclear family.

Invisible Grandmother

A brief but moving memoir of the self-effacing grandmother appeared as the *New York Times*' celebration of Mother's Day a year or so ago. "Bittersweet" was its title, but it was far more bitter than sweet as a ceremonial bow to motherhood and grandmotherhood. Its author, Martha Weinman Lear, recalled her grandmother, who lived with the family for twenty-five years, from her widowhood to the end of her long life.

Grandmother insisted upon doing the cooking, but she rarely ate with the family. Instead she ate her small meal quickly, well before the family's dinner hour, washed her dishes and vanished into her room. When her son-in-law came home in the evening she greeted him and disappeared. If she was in the room when dissension arose between the parents, or between parent and child, again she slipped away out of sight.

Her own mother, Mrs. Lear tells us, is also widowed, but she will not live with her daughter's family. She lives alone in another city. When she visits, she comes for two weeks, stays for one, and repeats her mother's pattern. She, too, is the invisible grandmother, a self-effacing shadow, and her humility fills her daughter with guilt—which inevitably becomes a helpless, irrational anger.

Well, you ask, what is a grandmother to do, in these days when she no longer has the support of tradition to give her status in her son's or daughter's house? When she feels she is an intruder, who is tolerated out of a sense of duty but has no value to the young family as a person?

And I must answer with my own questions. Who decides

that she is an intruder? Who makes the judgment that she is of no use to the young family? Isn't this something she does to herself? Haven't we learned long since that a person who does not value himself is not valued by anyone?

When that grandmother tried to make herself unseen and unheard, she was not less but more intrusive. She made the family more aware of her and more uncomfortable about her in her absence than she could possibly have done by sharing their ordinary life. She could not avoid having a relationship with them any more than she could dematerialize her physical presence. People who live under the same roof have a relationship whether or not they want it. The only question is its quality.

As to that, both sides contribute. A grandmother living in her grown child's house owes it to herself and to the family to do her part in making it work. Where the grandchildren are concerned, she is in the perfect spot for building a relationship—she does not have to invent it out of long-distance ingenuities as we absentee grandmothers do. But in her relationships with the parents, tradition or no tradition, she must create her own place and make her own justification for sharing the family's life, and she must do this even more in her own eyes than in theirs.

She may feel resentment from either her own child or her in-law child, but she would be wise to understand this as resentment toward the situation rather than toward herself. Very often, as we know, people accept an arrangement in good faith, but are not always able to accept the rubs that stem from it.

Whatever its first cause, resentment feeds on everyday irritations. A daughter-in-law complained to me, "I can't bear it when she cooks for us—she's a great cook and the food is wonderful, but she leaves me such a messy stove!" I asked, "Why don't you tell her?" and so she did. It turned out that Grandma didn't even see the mess she left until she overcame her vanity and took to wearing her glasses when she cooked.

Life with anyone, husband, parent, child, is full of these small annoyances, but they needn't be allowed to grow into chronic headaches. Grandma, for one, can't afford to cause them, but often she does not know that she does. In that case it was the daughter-in-law, with a nudge from a friend, who spoke up. But we can't count on our children to tell us their complaints against us. They are afraid of hurting our feelings, either because we are older, or because, as is true with many live-in grandmothers, we are dependent.

So it is up to us to set the tone of an open, candid relationship, first of all by showing that we are capable of it, that we welcome the give and take of equals—that we are not *touchy*! A forthright friendly "What's bothering you?" can elicit a long-standing if trivial complaint. And often the complaint is dissipated almost as soon as it is aired. The simple airing of it relieves the irritation, and once it has been discussed, both parties usually make an effort to accommodate.

The three-generation household is no longer a rose garden, if it ever was. One of the more successful arrangements is for grandmother to live with the family and yet separately by having her own small apartment within the family house.

People have found it possible to provide this even in modest houses in the suburbs or in a residential neighborhood in the city. In my own neighborhood in the heart of Manhattan, young parents have been rehabilitating the old brownstones for their growing families, usually with one or two independent apartments. I am told by a much traveled friend that in some parts of Europe the three-generation household has not been abandoned, but has been brought up to date with a separate apartment for the grandparents within the family dwelling—usually, because of inheritance customs, the eldest son's. That seems to offer the best of both worlds, closeness and independence neatly blended.

In our own culture, the live-in grandmother still needs to justify herself by good works. How can she be useful?

Useful Grandmother

Anyone would think that in the complicated life of a modern American family, a live-in grandmother would be beyond price.

In the single-parent household that is now becoming almost a commonplace, thanks to the high divorce rate, there is no doubt about her usefulness. The same is true in a family in which both parents are out of the house during much of the waking day, whether at work, in school, or pursuing some other interest. Even in a family where the wife—or the husband—is at home, a family with children can always use an extra pair of hands.

Why is it, then, that so much of what we read about in-house grandmothers is negative? Are successful live-in grandmothers like happy lives—nobody writes about them because there is nothing to tell?

Grandmother knows well enough how to be useful. The question is how to be useful without being interfering, or bossy, or in the way. To clean, to cook, to market, to watch the baby or toddler at home, to welcome the older ones when they come in from school or play—that's a mothering job, and a familiar one.

But in this house she is not mothering but grandmothering. The authority under this roof is not hers but the parents', and the house rules are not of her making but theirs. The live-in grandmother is constantly swinging between her old and new roles, between functioning at the hub of the family circle and sitting somewhere on the rim.

Take cooking. We used to say that no kitchen is big enough for two women, and now we have to include husbands and fathers at the cooking stove and the sink. That most important room in the house is getting crowded. Grandmother may be an accomplished cook and baker, but if one of the parents in the family has a positive passion for cooking, grandmother must stand aside and reserve her skill for the special occasions when it is wanted. She can make herself available so that she will be asked to take over on occasion, but she cannot automatically take the kitchen as her realm. It is not her kitchen.

It is the same with every other family task, from cleaning to marketing to baby care. No two people do these things the same way, and each of us likes her own way best. Grandmother can volunteer, but she cannot assume any of these jobs as her own.

Keeping the young children in order, disciplining the older ones, helping them with school work—or not doing any of these things—were all aspects of family life that she would take for granted as hers to deal with. But they are hers no longer, or they are hers only by the parents' leave.

So it is true, as live-in grandmothers and the families they live with have told me, that making oneself a useful grandmother in a son's or daughter's home is no open-and-shut proposition. It takes tact, and awareness, and a willingness to stand aside or step in as the need appears.

I think it also takes a degree of toughness, of resistance to being walked over. Successful grandmothers, old or new style, are not doormats. But neither are they autocrats. A family cannot love a grandmother who either imposes or is imposed upon. They can love a grandmother who knows herself to be a person in her own right, and does not need to be either dominating or dependent, either self-asserting or self-effacing. If she also has the gift of humor and a capacity for fun, she contributes to everyone's enjoyment of living, and not least her own.

Practical Grandmother

Experience teaches us that a good relationship, even an ideal one, has to have a practical foundation, and the first steps in undertaking life with the family are down-to-earth ones. Take money, for a start. It is the notorious troublemaker in families, mainly because it is almost never discussed openly at the outset. Generous gestures, loving offers—"You'll never have to worry about money while you're with us, Mother"—grandmother can welcome them with thanks but if she is wise she will push on to the nub of things, the actual money arrangements.

If she has her own money, she may want to contribute a share of the family expenses, or at least pay for her own keep. If her services in housekeeping and child care are needed and can be given in lieu of money, that should be clearly agreed upon. Whatever her financial resources, it is good practice to reserve some money for her own use, even if it is only a small share of her social security benefits. No adult should have to ask for pocket money.

If a grandmother's services are not actually needed, still she is part of the family, and even if she contributes financially she is not a paying guest. She surely wants to be useful, and so she should be. But let her be quite clear with the parents of the house about what tasks she undertakes to do. And let her not undertake more than she can do with relative ease and comfort, and some satisfaction in the use of her skills, whatever they may be. A woman who has always disliked housekeeping tasks, and may not even have been good at them in her own house, should certainly not volunteer to do them in her grown child's house—unless the family situation requires it. She may be better at raising vegetables in the backyard garden plot than at dealing with them in the kitchen. A woman with a green thumb can beautify the house with indoor plants and leave the vacuum cleaner and floor waxer to someone else, either another member of the family or a hired cleaner. The apportioning of family work usually has a variety of alternatives, and nobody, not grandmother or any other member, should be a candidate for martyrdom, which costs far more than any family relationship can afford.

And let's not underrate the grandmotherly contribution that is not capable of being measured in physical or monetary terms. She is, or can be, the mainstay of serenity in the house. She is at a stage of her life when she is no longer striving and driving, no longer struggling on her own or through a husband for security, recognition, achievement, whether on a job, as a wife, a mother, or whatever her goals may have been.

Grandmother has had her successes and her defeats, has found her satisfactions or modified her expectations. Which is not to say that she has necessarily given up her interests, her useful work whether paid for or not, her friendships and associations—surely not. It means only that what she wants, under her son's or daughter's roof, is to participate in a harmonious family life, and to do her part in the nurture and growth of her grandchildren. And in that she can play a quiet but highly creative role.

Storytelling

Taking a pinch of snuff, she would tell me marvelous stories whose heroes were chivalrous bandits, saints, forest animals and demons. Her manner of storytelling evoked tenderness and mystery as she put her face close to mine and fixed me with her big, believing eyes. Thus was the strength that was developing in me directly infused from her. The longer she spoke—or rather, chanted—the more melodious became the flow of her words. Listening to her gave me inexpressible pleasure.

When she had finished I begged for another, and this is an example of what I got: "Now an old goblin lives in the stove. Once he ran a splinter into his paw. As he rocked back and forth with the pain, he whined, 'I can't bear it, little mice, it hurts so much!' "

And she lifted her own foot in her hands and rocked it, comically screwing up her face as if she actually felt the pain.

The bearded, good-natured sailors would listen, too, and applauding the stories, would urge, "Give us another, grandma." And in reward they would invite us to supper with them. There they plied her with vodka and me with watermelon.

—*My Childhood*, by Maxim Gorky

8

Giving Presents

A toy? A book? Something to wear?

Giving presents to children is pure pleasure—or is it? Choosing what to give is no breeze, and it never was. We did hard thinking and even some research when we were parents, and as grandparents we find we have to be even more thoughtful and selective. Just giving something is not really satisfying. It has to be the right thing.

Some of us take the easy way, and I suppose we all do on occasion. There's the Texas grandmother who solved the question of her grandson's birthday present with the shortest possible long-distance call to her daughter in New York. "Take him down to F.A.O. Schwarz and buy him whatever he wants, just so it doesn't cost less than $500," she said.

Probably apocryphal, like most Texas stories—the $500 price tag is too pat to be true. Actually I see no harm in consulting the child, his parents, or both, especially when, for geographical or other reasons, we are not on intimate daily terms with him. How can we keep abreast of a child's changing interests, his unvoiced wishes? Certainly for the main events, the birthdays and Christmases and graduations, we need some inside information.

Parents are our surest source of guidance with a young

child—almost anything past the rattle and cuddly animal toy is pure guesswork unless we are with him day by day. What will keep him happy longest without company? When is it time for building blocks? The first puzzles? Manufacturers mark their toys as suitable for certain ages, but what do you make of a jigsaw puzzle labeled for ages four to ten? One day I bought three, one for the younger child, one for the older one, and one that I thought might interest either—only to be told by the seven-year-old, a puzzle whiz who had been doing jigsaws since she was three, that the baby puzzle turned out to be hard even for her. I have found that one cannot rely on manufacturers' or salespeople's judgment about what is right for what age, except within such a broad range that it is almost no help at all.

As grandmothers we have another, perhaps equally compelling reason for conferring with the children's parents. How often in our own child-raising years did we stand aghast at the messes of finger paints, clay, and workshop tools, the nuisance of bits and pieces of games strewn around the house, the booby-trap hazard of rocking horses and riding toys for which we had no space, the living room floor given over to block architecture, toy trains, toy farms? Granted that the children enjoy and grow with these toys. But many of our young families live in cramped quarters, and many young mothers work part or full time. Parents have to live with children's toys as well as with children, and parents' comfort is also a consideration.

Later come questions of street dangers—the tricycle, the roller skates, the first two-wheeler. What seems to us a right and timely present may raise other considerations, practical or worrisome, that we hadn't thought of. It would be a flighty grandmother indeed who would offer a major gift to a child without first consulting the child's parents.

Too Rich, Too Grand

In this connection I want to make a plea for grandmotherly (and grandfatherly) restraint. Our sons and daughters in the early years of their marriage may be stretching a modest income as far as it will go, and they do not have too much to spend on playthings for the children. They make careful choices of sturdy toys that will last, and often a dextrous and imaginative parent will improvise a toy rather than buy one.

How does a father or mother feel, after spending hours making a doll house out of an orange crate, when a large Christmas package arrives from Grandma that turns out to be a Southern mansion complete with pillared façade and rooms filled with period furniture?

Do I exaggerate? Consult your own conscience about the lavishness of some of your presents. Or, if you have not yielded to that temptation, remember some of your friends who have. Daughters and daughters-in-law have told me how the arrival of grandparents laden with gifts has turned the visit from a pleasure into a nervous tug of war over the too rich, too fancy feast of toys they bring with them—the elegant oversize doll that makes the rest of a child's doll family look shabby, the tremendous train set that sweeps all other possessions under the sofa. The parents stand wondering how they can deal with children in whom such expensive appetites have been aroused. And it does not help their feelings when even a mild protest is met with the injured response, "But it gives us such pleasure!"

It is a different matter when the child's parents acknowledge in advance that he would like an expensive toy they can't afford. Then the grandparental checkbook brings joy all around, and not dismay. Or, if $100, more or less, is burning a hole in your pocket, a consultation over what to spend it on is surely in order. It might buy a super swing set for the back yard that brings playmates to a child who needs them, or keeps the child under a hard-pressed mother's eye while she looks after the baby. It might buy a supply of toys to be spread out over months of surprises.

For a child who is ready for painting, it might buy an entire miniature studio package—easel, sturdy brushes, a dozen jars of poster paints, an ample supply of newsprint, plus a smock for the child and a square of heavy oil cloth to spread on the floor for easy cleaning up. For a reading-writing child it might buy a first typewriter, and for a musical child a good record player of his own and a first collection of records. A more sizable sum could buy the family their first piano (my choice would be a small upright, secondhand but expertly examined for structural soundness) with a check to cover the piano tuner's fee and the child's first music lessons. Or ballet lessons, riding lessons, accessories included.

Some families are so situated that they can accept a pony, if not a horse. I knew some children whose greatest delight was their grandmother's gift of a pet goat. A small pet may be acceptable, or a rabbit family in the yard, or an aquarium.

One simple but marvelous summer present a friend once gave my children was a caterpillarium. It was nothing more than a box made of rectangles of plate glass taped at the corners, with a lid that could be raised and three or four caterpillars resting and feeding on a leafy branch inside. The children kept them supplied with fresh branches of the same kind, and watched them through their metamorphoses. Then came the day when the butterflies emerged, one by one, each from its chrysalis—what a day that was! To carry each one on its branch carefully and tenderly out of doors, and watch it slowly spread its trembling, fragile wings to dry, then soar away into the sun—it was a day the children never forgot (nor did I). We can scarcely guess what precious residue such an intimate experience with one of nature's miracles can leave in a growing, expanding mind. (But make sure the children's parents do not mind small, crawly creatures.)

Surely when grandmother wants to spend money, she can find enough productive ways to spend it for her grandchildren. But it is just as certain that no important present, one that involves parents in its need for space or time or continued attention, can be given without consulting with them beforehand.

Everyday Toys

With the casual everyday toys we have a relatively free hand, but even there we can do with some considered thought. Nobody needs to be warned nowadays that plastic toys may break and leave sharp edges, that small objects can get into mouths and noses, that painted toys must be certified lead-free and plushy toys should be marked fire-resistant. We learned long ago to read the fine print and spot toxic ingredients, and the government gives us a little more help than in the past with its labeling regulations.

We should remember also that a toy too advanced for a particular child's stage of development may be challenging, but can also lead to frustrated rage—and on the other hand that one too young for him is of no interest at all, a total waste. He can grow up to a too advanced toy but he cannot be squeezed into a too babyish one, any more than he can be squeezed into clothes he has outgrown. The too advanced toy can always be put away in the closet for a later time.

In our younger, more frugal days we used to watch for toys that, like some books, would interest a child at different levels as he grew older. Good building blocks are the perfect example. So are modular communities which can be put up in a variety of ways. So are an easel and paints, modeling clay, construction toys of various kinds. There are also the sturdy toddler toys that can be handed down to the next child.

There are some games that offer similar elasticity, such as Monopoly, and some new games that catch the current issues, such as Survival and Ecology. Magic sets can begin simply (there are some fifty kits on the market, so choose carefully) and the child can go on to greater complexities, even to patronizing the magic specialty shops.

There are games that you can play with your grandchildren—and that you can lose without trying. One that used to be called Blockhead involved building with odd-shaped blocks, and the player whose tower first tottered and fell was the blockhead. Another that is still current in toy catalogues, called Memory, is a deck of about a hundred small cards that are spread out face down, looked at one by one, and replaced. When a card is turned up that matches another, the player must try to remember where the matching card is. Children easily challenge us in the patient manual skill that one of these requires, and the visual memory needed for the other.

Our grandchildren are more sophisticated than our own children were at the same ages, thanks to television, nursery schools, and generally more knowledgeable parents—there has been a vast amount of parent education going on, conscious and unconscious, in these intervening twenty years or so. Our sons and daughters and in-laws may also be more issue-oriented than we were. They may have strong feelings against guns and war toys, or about dolls and toy kitchenware being suited only for girls. Daddies as well as Mommies cook and clean these days, and many fathers are as good at diapering and bathing and feeding the baby as mothers ever were. (There is even a delightful children's book about this by Charlotte Zolotow, *William's Doll*, in which grandmother comes to the rescue, buys William the doll he yearns for, and explains to the boy's embarrassed father that this is how William will learn to be a good father like him.)

Grandmother has her options. She can always put a truck instead of a tank into her grandson's hands. And if bringing him a baby doll is just too much of a departure for her, she can duck the sex role question and bring him a building set. But she will have to conceal her surprise at finding him tenderly tucking his sister's baby doll into bed, if sister permits, or at seeing his sister sawing and hammering with his new tool set.

She must also hide her disappointment if the toy she chose as just the thing for the particular child is met with a total lack of interest. Or if the brand-new doll's head is parted from its body an hour later, or the building set scattered and its parts broken. Children can be rough and destructive even with a beloved grandmother's gifts, unless the gift fits into a child's special interest of the moment. A beautiful doll can mean less than nothing to a child of the wrong age, or of a different taste.

One of the ways to avoid instant destruction is to choose for sturdiness, especially for the nursery and kindergarten ages. The money we spend for good construction is not wasted—like good clothes, durable toys can be passed on. A grandmother who should have known better (meaning myself) was hooked twice, first by a record player that she was assured a three-year-old could play, then by a typewriter that was sold as usable for a five-year-old (my grandchildren have a mother who writes, working at home). Both were plausible plastic imitations of the real thing, and neither of them worked for longer than a week. And they were not cheap either, needless to say.

We used to know brand names we could trust, but even those are not automatically trustworthy anymore. Many of our old reliables have been bought by conglomerates and their manufacturing standards have been watered down. So in the end we must go and look and decide for ourselves over every separate purchase, until we know what the present score is and can trust the illustrations in the catalogues.

This is not necessarily an unadulterated chore. There are nostalgic joys as well as some pleasant surprises in toylands revisited.

With all this, your best friend may yet be the shopping bag of expendable toys you have collected here and there against your next visit to the children—the knickknacks and odd little objects that are of no account, need not be handled with care, and lend themselves to an hour of fun. Balloons, dime store balls, yo-yos, tops, pipe-cleaner figures, silly animals, funny stickers, Mexican jumping beans, puzzles, tricks, false noses, funny faces, funny hats—in this grab bag anything goes. A treasure trove for a rainy day.

As They Get Older

As the children get older their special interests become more marked, and gifts become easier to choose. Our emerging stamp collector knows what stamps he needs to fill out his series and our rock specialist knows his minerals. We need only ask him.

But here, too, there are hazards. One grandmother asked a grandson what he wanted for his seventeenth birthday. An electric guitar, he told her. A biggish investment, but almost any grandmother who got this request from a child across the continent would feel that she had to grant it, if it was something she could afford. Fortunately this grandmother was not separated from the young family by any vast distance. She saw the children often enough to know that, although this boy liked his generation's music as well as the next teen-ager, he was not a budding musician. So she asked a question or two, and within minutes the boy said, "Well, I guess what I really want is some parts for the car I'm building." With that, the conversation got down to practical matters of how much money would buy what part, and grandmother sent a check for the agreed amount.

This nice child was apparently shy of asking his grandmother straight out for anything so crass as money. Other, often unguessed, inhibitions may hamper other young people when we ask, "What do you want?" If we suspect that the birthday or graduating child is not the best guide, we have other reliable sources of information. Parents, or perhaps at this age a sibling, may have knowledge of some private yearning we cannot elicit by ourselves.

Presents to teen-age and older grandchildren can be expensive. In another chapter we talk about money, and how important it is for children to know our financial situation. When children know an unalterable reality they accept it, and Joey, whose grandmother told me this story, showed that they can also be considerate. It was a question of his high school graduation present, and after much conversation back and forth he wistfully confessed that what he would really like was a trip to visit a favorite uncle in a distant city. This meant an outlay of perhaps $150, and his grandmother's major gifts were generally about a third of that. But Grandma felt that such a trip would mean a great deal to both her grandson and her son, the boy's uncle, and that it would nurture those good family feelings we all long for. So she said that when the time came for him to buy his ticket she would send him a check for the fare.

Joey did not leave it at that. He knew without being told that such a graduation present was a large expenditure for Grandma, and it troubled him enough so that he discussed it with his mother. When he was ready to buy his ticket he told his grandmother on the phone, "Send only half—Mother will pay the other half."

Our grandchildren are not only considerate—they will also accommodate. This time it is a granddaughter story. Allison also wanted a special kind of present. She wanted to be taken along on her grandmother's next trip abroad. Allison was very much an undergraduate and she followed campus style to the last negligent detail. On visits home she arrived in ragged jeans, a sloppy sweatshirt, her long hair loose and unkempt, and her belongings in a backpack. Her grandmother is small, trim, and very correct in all her ways including the way she dresses.

Despite their striking differences—in philosophies as well as clothes—she and Allison have always been good friends, and when Allison asked to go along on a trip her grandmother was genuinely delighted—with one reservation. "But not the way you look," said grandmother. "Right on!" said Allison, or whatever the campus response of the moment may have been. And when the time came to take off, Allison's hair was trimmed, brushed, and shining, and she was dressed in the kind of clothes she had been brought up to wear. She also carried a conventional handbag and had packed a conventional suitcase. Nothing needed to be said on either side. Allison had simply accommodated to her grandmother's sensibilities, and they set off for their holiday together in high spirits.

We sometimes feel we do all the bending to our young people's ways. Not so. They will bend, too.

Pictures and Words

Surprises await us when we begin buying books for our grandchildren. Times have changed, and taste and pace are very different from our children's young days, let alone ours. The books being offered to children reflect the changes, not always admirably. Cruelty, violence, cynicism, pornography have crept in from the adult world.

It is all very well to argue that children need to learn what the real world is like, but reality has many faces, hopeful and wholesome as well as ugly and unsavory. Books in which all the adults are mean and evil do not accurately reflect reality, and the four-letter words that have found their way into some books for children are already obsolete, as at least one critic has vigorously observed. It is one thing for a child to sneak a look at a book whose chief recommendation is its sensationalism—didn't we all? It is quite another thing for such a book to be handed to a child by a loving adult with the implication that it is something he will like.

Whatever the theorists may say about children's need to have all the information about everything, grandmother still has her options. She does not have to give a child a book that someone else says is good for him. She can give him one that she thinks is a good book.

All the same, we do have to take the changing times into account. Most of us discovered with our own children that our childhood favorites were not necessarily theirs. If you remember trying to read them with your boy or girl back then, you will also remember your discovery that you had to skip pages and gloss over passages at a dizzying rate to keep the child's interest. Was it *Gulliver's Travels*, *Robinson Crusoe*, *The Water Babies*, *Wind in the Willows*, in which you found long, indigestible paragraphs and even some nightmare horrors that you had forgotten? Those were books of social criticism, not children's books, even though many of us read them as children.

Would you read "The Little Match Girl" or "The Red Shoes" to your young grandchildren at bedtime? Even *Peter*

Pan, with its menacing Captain Hook, may be a bit much for some children to go to sleep on. Granted that youngsters enjoy scary stories, and some of them want their entertainment full of gore. I prefer to follow the old copy editor's rule, "When in doubt—out," and leave the rough or dubious stories for them to read for themselves when they are old enough to choose their own reading matter.

How do *you* choose? The picturebook age is relatively easy. We can stand at the book counter and run through half a dozen of them in a few minutes. That doesn't mean we should suspend judgment—by no means. Children of whatever age are entitled to good, well-written stories, however slender the text, and to good quality pictures in their picturebooks. We need not settle for easy commercial art, or poor taste, or unimaginative color and design. Some excellent artists are devoting their talent to children's books, and we only need to compare one with another to see the differences in quality. And when we choose funny books, let's be sure they are funny to children, not just to their parents. Too much humor in children's books trades on an adult sophistication far beyond a child's level of laughter.

As they get older, the array of storybooks and fact books is bewildering. We could not plow through a fraction of them, supposing we had time to do so, without perishing of sheer exhaustion. Let the children's book critics do that job for us. Not that I would trust just any book reviews for my grandchildren's books, any more than I would for my own. Critics, too, have their blind spots—or their prejudices—and I like to know who is telling me about a book.

There are other sources of information about new children's books. Every librarian has the American Library Association's list of recommended books. The Child Study Association of America publishes a selective listing of each year's new books on which an entire committee of knowledgeable parents of varying ages have agreed. Then there is the *Hornbook*, the literary magazine of the children's book world, published quarterly. The American Association for the Advancement of Science publishes a children's book review bulletin, a sound guide of science books from A for anthropology to Z for zoology.

Librarians consult these and other sources when buying books for their shelves, and you and I can well consult the librarians. A visit to the children's room of your public library, or to your school library if it is accessible, will give you the benefit of the librarian's selection for a start. If you have further questions, most librarians are inclined to be helpful if we catch them at a slack time of day. Or you can ask to see some of the review sources that the librarian consults.

How far any grandmother wants to go in making book choices, how much time she is able or willing to spend, depends on how much she cares about giving her grandchildren books. We all want them to read and enjoy books, but the books we give them are not the only books they get. For many of us, the picturebooks and the first storybooks are about as much as we can manage with any feeling of security, and later an occasional fact or science or how-to book that seems to fit into an older grandchild's special interest. And we need not limit ourselves to the standard children's bookshelves. I have discovered that a book of Audubon bird and animal prints and a museum catalogue of American folk art can fascinate some children of the picturebook age. A vast amount of fine art speaks to all ages, not just to adults.

One development borrowed from the adult book world is a special boon to grandmothers—the paperback. With the price of children's books today it was probably inevitable. But the beauty of paperbacks for us is not only their low cost but their portability. We can mail them in an ordinary manila envelope, stuff them by the half dozen in the suitcase when we go visiting, dump them in the shopping bag with the other expendable knickknacks we pick up on a shopping jaunt in town.

Many of the children's paperbacks are reprints of the best picture-storybooks we had for our own children, timeless books by gifted artist-writers that are as enjoyable today as they were then. Others are reading books for the school-age child, sometimes reprints and sometimes new books. Book-minded grandmothers can only give thanks for this blessing.

When it comes to reprints, whether in hard or soft covers, watch for the words "edited" or "adapted." Publishers and editors have boiled down many classics, hoping to make the great children's books of the past attractive to impatient or reluctant young readers today. In some of these the editing has been limited to judicious cutting. Others have been more or less rewritten, preserving the story if not the style.

There are precedents for this in literature. Charles Lamb gave us tales from Shakespeare and Nathaniel Hawthorne wrote memorable versions of the Greek myths for us. Conservatives may ask whether *Robinson Crusoe* by any hand but Daniel Defoe's is still *Robinson Crusoe*, and whether a single word can be spared from *Alice in Wonderland*. Dyed-in-the-wool classicists say that if children won't read these great books in the original perhaps they shouldn't read them at all.

A controversial question, and we can take our choice of either side. We cannot make children read the books we would like them to read. We can only offer, and hope our offering will be welcome.

One more point, an odd one. Children often ask for a book they have already read. This seems wasteful, but on second thought, why not? It is obviously a book the child likes, and wants to own and read again and again. So give it to him!

For the Record Player

If we are surprised at the variety of books for children, we will be staggered by the array of recordings. The standard catalogue, Schwann's Children's Record and Tape Guide, lists more than 1400 records and tapes for the young and teen years, and recorded music is only one segment of this vast listening library. For a child who is better at listening than reading, something to put on the turntable or the tape recorder may be a happy present.

As with books, records are easiest to choose for the young. Fine actors have made recordings of Mother Goose and of favorite children's stories. For example, Julie Harris and Louis Jourdan read the Babar stories, with M. Jourdan supplying the French accent. Mary Poppins is interpreted by Maggie Smith as the magical nanny. Claire Bloom reads stories from Beatrix Potter. Siobhan McKenna tells the life of Hans Christian Anderson and reads his poems, which children who know his stories might like to hear.

Then we come to the school-age classics. Anthony Quayle reads *Swiss Family Robinson* and also (for some children) *Don Quixote*. Basil Rathbone reads Sherlock Holmes, and Boris Karloff reads Kipling. Among authors interpreting their own works are Tolkien reading his Hobbit tales and T. S. Eliot reading *Old Possom's Practical Cats*.

And now the choosing of records for a grandchild becomes a challenge. The multiplicity of talking records will stop you in your tracks. There are documentaries, plays, history, poetry, language records, even a course in Morse Code. Your grandchild's interests by now have widened, or narrowed, as the case may be, to some specialty dear to the child's heart. Either you know what that absorbing special interest is—or you ask. How awkward to give a child a recording of bird songs in a suburban back yard, which you know and love, when the nature music your youngster has been reading about is the singing of whales or wolves! No problem, all are recorded, but you have to know which is wanted.

With a clue to the children's individual interests you can spring some delightful surprises. For children who enjoy being a little scared, "Spooky Sounds" is one of a number of sound-effect records now available, and for a youngster whose fancy wanders happily in outer space there is a record of "Sounds of Science Fiction" and another of "The War of the Worlds."

An eye-opening—or ear-opening—collection of old radio shows may please young listeners whose only experience of air-wave entertainment is television, and incidentally may bring a nostalgic echo of their young years to the children's parents. For those same youngsters who like scary stories are the *Green Hornet* and the *Creaking Door*, unrivalled radio purveyors of vicarious chills. The enduring humor of Fred Allen, Jack Benny, Fanny Brice, from radio's great days, can still be funny to modern teen-agers.

Music is still another matter. We cannot make them listen, any more than we can make them read. What we can do is expose them to our taste, with utmost tact, and hope that something will catch their interest. First of all there are the nostalgic records. Recently the young people have begun to rediscover the great age of jazz, and of even older ragtime. They have heard, or heard of, Scott Joplin and Eubie Blake, the ragtime pianists, and the jazz pianists like Fats Waller, Jelly Roll Morton, Teddy Wilson, Duke Ellington.

Great men, and the young people who hear them recognize their greatness. There are recordings of the stars of the big band era—Tommy Dorsey, Glenn Miller, Benny Goodman, including the memorable (to parents and grandparents) Benny Goodman concert in Carnegie Hall, recorded on the spot in 1938.

The music records have an exhaustive range, from folk music old and new to the full symphony repertoire. We used to introduce young childern to the symphony with works like Haydn's *Surprise Symphony* and *Clock Symphony*, and we still can. But now there is also Prokofiev's *Peter and the Wolf*, which delights all children, and for an older child his witty *Classical Symphony*, and perhaps for a still older child his *Lieutenant Kije*, full of Russian folk themes and with a clear anti-war message.

A grandchild who has had some exposure to the orchestra might like one of the recordings that introduce the sounds of the instruments one by one, like Benjamin Britten's *Young Person's Guide to the Orchestra*—and there are others. And for a child who is actually playing an instrument and has achieved some proficiency at it, there are recordings from the classical repertoire with one instrument missing—Mozart's Clarinet Quintet, for example, without the clarinet, so that your clarinetist grandchild can play the part for his instrument with accomplished professional musicians.

And what if your grandchild has neither played nor heard nor wants to hear anything but the cliché youth music, the folk-rock-country musical spectrum? The chances are that you don't know your way among those recordings, supposing that you can abide them at all. I am told that there are good quality music and musicians even in that jungle of commercialism and instant best sellers. As one of our own youth heroes, Duke Ellington, used to say, there are only two kinds of music, good and bad. I, for one, love the Beatles, what I have heard of them. If you know which is which in the young people's music world, you need no help from me.

But if you are as anti-rock as most of us grandparents seem to be, still all is not lost. There are unexpected links from that music to music we know and love. Interestingly, the links do not lead to the romantic 19th century music of our young years. I have not heard of teen-agers falling in love with Tchaikovsky. But a sixteen-year-old rock fan I know asked for some Bach organ music for Christmas last year. The elegantly structured baroque music, Bach and pre-Bach, Purcell, Bull, does have an appeal for them. The harpsichord and classical guitar also have something for them —perhaps it is the small, precise sound, a contrast to the indiscriminate decibels of their usual fare. They will even listen to Renaissance music on the old instruments, the viols and recorders. For these young explorers there is some very sophisticated Bach in jazz versions, and some electronic versions made with Moog synthesizers. From there it is not far to late Stravinsky, and young avant-garde composers of today.

If your young people are immersed in American folk music, some American program music might please them, such as Aaron Copland's ballet scores, *Rodeo* and *Billy the Kid*, which are filled with American West folk themes. And for the jazz fanciers, there is Leonard Bernstein's jazzy World War II sailors-on-shore-leave frolic, *Fancy Free*. And let's not forget Charles Ives, whose symphonic collages of American small town bands, parades, and popular music of his time, fifty and more years ago, are as electrifying as any newer music the young people are likely to hear.

With records as with books, for our young grandchildren we can take a chance and do the choosing. But for the older ones it is fatal to choose unless we truly know the direction of their tastes. Ask them what they want. And if you don't like it, given them something other than a record, or give them money. I don't know about you, but I like to *like* what I give them as presents.

Something to Wear

Grandmothers used to specialize in exquisite hand-embroidered baby clothes, frilly little-girl dresses, expensive small-boy suits. Those days are long gone. We may still have a yearning to see our grandchildren dressed up like little dolls, but their mothers prefer them in sturdy play clothes that come out of the washer-dryer ready to wear again. There is no one to stand over an ironing board anymore, ironing out all the ruffles and bows.

The same interchange with grown-ups has happened with clothes as with books, only in reverse. In clothes the adult world has borrowed from the playground, and we are all wearing some version of practical play clothes. We grannies in our trimly tailored, permanent press pants suits can hardly offer our grandchildren frills and furbelows—with one happy exception. Our girl children still adore a pretty party dress, and to our delight these now come in washer-dryer materials that need no ironing.

Buying clothes for children has changed in another way. These days even a toddler goes along on the shopping trip. They are making their own choices at earlier and earlier ages, and this goes for boys as well as girls. A three-year-old makes his own selection of the pajamas with the space ship on the chest, the T shirt with the football emblem. Even their mother does not make the decisions about what to wear—she can only guide them.

When grandmother buys a gift of clothing she does well to keep up to the minute in the fashions from teens all the way to nursery school. And she had also best take account of what the going thing is in the particular toddler set her youngster plays with, as well as the particular youngster's preferences of the moment.

The shortcut through all this is of course to make a shopping trip one of the events on a visit, and to go armed with careful instructions from the children's mother on what to steer the young ones away from as well as toward.

With clothes as with toys, labels are important. Everything has to be washable-dryable and allergies must be considered, if they exist, when you are buying those cosy pajamas, nightgowns, and warm fluffy robes.

Add considerations of size, fit, comfort, durability, becomingness—and grandmother's pocketbook. Children today readily understand and accept all these criteria, including getting good value for Grandma's money. (Or they do if the matter of money has been realistically dealt with; see Chapter 9.)

What to do if a child's heart becomes set on something really unsuitable? Grandmother always has a way out—she says, "Let's wait and ask Mother." Or, if her personal taste is involved, there is no reason why she can't say—since it is true—"When I give someone a present, I like to like it, too." And there is a value in telling a child what you like—it may not change her taste that moment but eventually it may have an influence.

One final caveat. Spare yourself and the children, but especially yourself, by not undertaking too long a shopping list, and break it with a sit-down snack. Nothing is fun when people are tired.

Some of us dote on shopping and find it a kind of recreation. But more women dislike it than anyone, particularly any man, believes. And many of us, whether or not we enjoy it, have cut it to the essential minimum in order to have time for other things. But somehow shopping with our grandchildren has a different savor. Any other kind of shopping may be a burdensome chore, but with a child who is interested—and not every child is—it becomes an adventure. The child's own pleasure in seeking and choosing infuses the whole experience with a glow.

And there is always that further value, so precious to those of us who are absentee grandmothers for much of the year, of getting to know and be known to our grandchild. Remembering this, we discover that a shopping trip can be a good one even if it is not successful in terms of what we bring home. Even the disappointment of not finding a particular item the child is hunting for is a shared disappointment, and if Grandma genuinely shares it, that too is a further strengthening of our bond.

With it all, a hot fudge sundae before we head for home can transform any excursion into a success.

Grandma Crafts

Grandmother craftswomen are the particular beneficiaries of the fashions, right now as I write. Everything can be knitted, crocheted, tricked out with emblems, patches, slogans, bleached or dipped or painted or tie-dyed or batiked, whatever may be your particular skill. Those of us who knit and crochet have always made baby blankets, sweaters, socks, mittens, bonnets. Nowadays the demand for our handiwork runs right up through the teens and twenties, and it goes from hats and minimum sleeveless tops that take almost no time to make, to cable-stitched and popcorn-popping sweaters, ponchos, scarves, shawls, skirts short and long, even high-fashion coats. Grandmothers need never sit with idle hands.

There used to be jokes about clothes made by loving hands at home—and looking it. Today no one is inept who wants to learn. Yarn and needlework shops have sprouted in neighborhoods and shopping centers, with an eager teacher in every one of them. Friends of mine who haven't held a crochet hook since they learned at their mother's knee have taken it up again, to please a grandchild who wants a perky cap or cape.

I know of no pleasure that quite matches that of seeing your youngster proudly flaunting something you have made. No matter if it goes out of fashion and into a drawer next season, never to be seen again, you've had your reward. As long as grandma crafts remain in the ascendant, let's make the most of them.

My Grandmother's Domain

The only one in the house who wasn't afraid of [Grandfather] was my small and peppery grandmother with the corners of her silk headkerchief always fluttering under her chin. "Who do you think he is, the Tsar?" she berated her eldest son as he paced back and forth working up his nerve to face his father. "Go on in, he won't spank you. . . ."

Just as in Grandfather's court room, many women also gathered in my grandmother's domain, the kitchen, to pour out their troubles and joys, to voice their problems and difficulties. I frequently stole out of Grandfather's study to witness the doings in the female portion of the house. . . .

The household she supervised was always swarming with people. . . . She was never off her feet, skipping from closet to cupboard to pantry with swift, lively steps, her keys jangling, as she kept coming back to the huge stove where something was always cooking or baking.

—*Of a World That Is No More*,
by Isaac Bashevis Singer

9

Speaking of Money

It is absurd to be delicate on the subject of money. We live in a money-centered society, and however much or little of it may be involved, money finds its way into every relationship. Not to deal with it openly and plainly as a fact of our lives is to invite misunderstandings, resentments, grief, and pain. It is a more crucial subject for us as grandmothers than perhaps we recognize, or want to recognize.

I have before me one of those social science type studies of the role of grandparents today, and it speaks of areas of conflict, saying, "Money may be the most galling of them all."

In part the money situation is forced on us. When our children marry while they are still in school, there is no help for it but to subsidize them as far as we can. If babies are born we have no choice. As my friend Addie said, "There they are, both still in college, and no money even to buy milk for the baby—what can you do?"

Trouble comes when the subsidy goes on and on, when children who are now parents are still dependent, when grandchildren discover—or are told—that not their parents but their grandparents are supporting them, and when grandparents begin to use money as power. If we are tempted to pull the money strings, we would do better to cut them entirely and let our children make their own way.

But it need not be a case of either-or—either we support them and run their lives, or we turn our backs and do not help at all. I have talked to many grandmothers, some who live on ample incomes, some who have small ones, and some who still work for a living, and I find there are any number of ways of helping our young families without either taking control of them or making them dependent.

Some Good Old Ways

Some of these ways are traditional, and we are all familiar with them. We see our children through college, through graduate school as well, if we can. This can still be the rule, even if they marry. In one young couple's case, the groom's parents continued to pay his bills and the bride's parents continued to pay hers. As I remember that situation, the young people strove to save their parents some of the expense by thrifty management and pick-up jobs along the way. Good will on both sides helps mightily.

Other standard forms of grandmotherly subsidy are day-care help, nursery school, private kindergarten, summer camp if it is wanted, private schooling if it is desirable and within grandparents' means. None of these forms of assistance carries with it a grant of authority over how the money is spent.

One of the nicest stories I was told was of grandparents who sternly disapproved of progressive schools—"The children play all day and never learn anything." But when their daughter chose a famous New York City progressive school for their grandchildren, they paid the tuition without a murmur. They may have been convinced that the school would ruin their grandchildren for life (I suspect grandfather did so believe) but the children's mother was the one to decide and that was that. Note: The grandchildren did learn, and one of them is a physician and an admirable mother, and the other is a distinguished architect and an exceptional father. Even grandfather would have to admit he had made a good investment.

One family has a long tradition of grandparents paying the grandchildren's allowance while they are in college. My friend, now a grandmother herself, recalls the $10 a week from her grandmother which was generous in her undergraduate days. Her own grandchildren's expenses are several times as much, but she has no intention of breaking the tradition.

Buying a House

Grandparents also traditionally chip in, if they can, to help the parents of their grandchildren buy a house. Young parents rarely have the cash for a down payment, and they may or may not have the credit standing for a mortgage, so the older generation not infrequently comes to the rescue. Whatever they contribute, they may make the sum a gift, a loan, or an investment. But no matter what they call it, it is an investment, usually a substantial one. And here I think another grandmother friend of mine was entirely correct when she declined to put money into a house that she thought was a poor buy. Note that this is different from a choice of schools, on which parents may well be more knowledgeable than grandparents, if only because they are more up-to-date. On investments the older generation has the inestimable advantage of experience.

It happened that she was both experienced and knowledgeable, and probably she was right. Mind you, she did not tell her daughter and son-in-law not to buy it. She simply said she would not help, and she told them why. Whether or not they agreed with her, her arguments gave them pause. They looked further, and when they found a house that she thought was a good enough investment she willingly provided the down payment.

Another grandmother simply gave her children the down payment as a gift, no questions asked, and that was her prerogative. Still another grandmother, who has limited resources as her children know, volunteered the down payment and a sum for house improvement, and her contribution is understood to be a kind of family mortgage without interest, to be paid back at some future time or out of the price the house brings if it is eventually sold. And if she has no need for the money at that time, she always has the option of making it a gift, or of offering it to her children to apply to the next house they buy, or the college expense of a grandchild, or whatever seems desirable then.

Gift? or Loan?

All the arrangements I have mentioned are clear understandings and there is nothing about any of them that is likely to cause grief. We and our children—and our grandchildren—need to be specific about the difference between a gift and a loan. A loan is something to be paid back, and I see no embarrassment in asking a child or a grandchild who wants a loan, "How are you planning to pay it back?" It is, after all, part of their education for living in the real world, and if we who love them won't teach them what they need to know, we may be leaving them to learn in some very unpleasant ways.

On the other hand, there is nothing to stop us from forgiving a loan when the child is ready to pay it back. We can say—if it is true—that we don't need that money right now, and offer to put it toward something that the young person needs or would like. My point is only that these exchanges should always be clear and businesslike, because if they are not, the unloving emotions that can result are far from worth the money that is involved.

They Know the Score

By the time they are old enough to be aware of money, our grandchildren have a rather clear idea of our financial status —we don't have to spell it out. They know whether grandmother lives on her social security, or a pension, or has a cushiony income from stocks and bonds. They know when grandmother works for a living and whether she budgets her trips and visits.

They begin to draw the distinctions very early. A four-year-old said to her grandmother, "Grandma Alice gives us lots of things and money to spend, but you take us to such nice places." The places she was talking about were the park, the carousel, the zoo, the museums, most of them free, but that did not diminish their value to the child. This grandmother might not give her money to spend, but she gave time and attention and shared enjoyment.

And why shouldn't the children know what we can and cannot afford? They don't measure our worth to them in terms of presents and material things (although, to be sure, they love opening all the little packages!) and neither should we. Only insecure people feel the need to buy love with anything but love. I have always believed firmly that richer is better, and money is something you can't have too much of. But money can be a double-edged sword in family relationships.

Even if Grandma is loaded, as an older child might put it, she can arrange matters so that money need never be an issue. A friend whose family fortune is one of the famous ones in America put it in her own way. She said, "None of my children turned out to be money-makers. One is an archeologist, another a professor of economics—you get the picture. So I made trusts for the grandchildren. They can pay for their own prep schools, colleges, graduate schools. They can even pay for having their teeth straightened!"

Those "non-money-making" sons and daughters and the grandchildren as well will have no money problems when the time comes to inherit. But meanwhile grandmother lives at peace with them all, and her acknowledged wealth creates no dissension. Compare this with the way another rich grandmother, Sara Delano Roosevelt, doled out allowances to her grown son and his grown sons, giving them instructions, along with the money, on how they should manage their lives. Franklin Delano Roosevelt's mother was a matriarch out of another era, when perhaps a woman with so much drive for power had no other channel for it but her family. We no longer need to aspire to the matriarch's role.

Another friend of mine, a superb businesswoman who made her own fortune, did the grandmotherly thing in her own way. She made her two married daughters partners in her business, which paid them incomes at a time when their husbands were just getting started. Then when she thought the time was ripe to cut them loose, she bought them out at the actual value of their partnerships. This came to quite a substantial sum for each, and gave them money of their own to manage in their own way. That, too, has worked out happily for the young families, giving them help when they needed it and independence when they were ready for it.

Not So Businesslike

If it is hard to be businesslike about money with our children, it is surely next to impossible with our grandchildren. Suppose, as happened to one grandmother, the children want to give their parents an anniversary present, and even by pooling their savings they are several dollars short. Will Grandma lend them the difference? They will pay it back out of their allowances. Grandmother knows what their allowances are, and she can just see herself being repaid, week by week, in nickels, dimes, and quarters. No doubt that would be a sound learning experience for the children. But can we blame her if she says, "Oh, no, let this be my part of the present!"?

We grannies are a soft-hearted lot, all too ready to take the same position with them at twenty and twenty-five as we did when they were ten and fifteen. It is absolutely predictable. An otherwise money-sensible grandmother was enjoying a visit from her college senior granddaughter, and from another room she heard granddaughter crying over the phone, talking to her boyfriend. The tears were because boyfriend didn't have the fare to come down for Christmas. How much? asked grandmother—$45, replied granddaughter. "Oh, I can give you that for his fare," said grandmother, and so she did.

When the family gathered at Christmas, the young man quite properly thanked grandmother for the loan and said he would pay it back, although it might take a while. "Oh, no," said grandmother, "that was my Christmas present to you both."

Was she wrong? It was not a large sum of money, to be sure, but there was a principle involved, and as we like to say, it isn't the money, it's the principle, right? A present is something we ordinarily buy, or make—or at least choose. Strictly speaking, the money for that airplane ticket should have been a loan, not a gift.

But at the risk of contradicting everything I have said in this chapter—or nearly everything—about money, I'm not sure it is bad for our grandchildren to know that there is at least one person in their lives who doesn't have to discipline them, who doesn't need to tell them what to do or not to do, who can give them both love and money without strings attached.

Giving and Bequeathing

A friend once told me of a bevy of grannies, in the town where she spent her childhood, whose greatest delight was to get together of an afternoon and talk about their wills. Nothing entertained them more than to make imaginary distributions and redistributions of their property and possessions among their children and grandchildren, rewarding this one and rebuking that one with the generosity or the stinginess of each one's share.

An odd choice of entertainment, no doubt. But we do think about our grandchildren's future and how best we can contribute to it. And we think about our possessions, and which of them would give most pleasure to which of our children and grandchildren.

One grandmother, who must be one of many, decided that she wanted to see her gifts enjoyed, and so she divided a part of her small savings among her daughter and her two grandchildren. Her grandson, whose family was growing, used his share as down payment on a house. Her granddaughter spent hers on a glorious vacation trip abroad with her husband and children. Her daughter and son-in-law built a porch on their summer home, which the family instantly christened Grandma's Porch. Rocking on the porch they had named for her, listening to her grandson's description of his new house and her granddaughter's account of the trip abroad, that grandmother had her wish, sharing the pleasures she had had it in her power to bestow.

I am told that there are legitimate ways in which we can all make such gifts and see them enjoyed, up to $3,000 a year, to as many different persons as we choose, without the gifts being subject to tax. We can also make larger gifts, to a total of $30,000 during our lifetime, also tax-exempt. There are correct ways to set up trusts for our grandchildren that will not be subject to estate tax, and to designate items of our possessions for them that we can continue to enjoy meanwhile, which also will not be part of the taxable estate. We can make gifts of securities, and in some states also of money, to our grandchildren who are still minors, under a variety of forms, some of which are legally exempt from estate taxes.

All these gifts can of course be taken care of in an ordinary will. Sums and securities can be placed in testamentary trust for children who may still not have reached their legal majority, and personal effects can be itemized as bequests to those who are to have them.

But those of us who would like to spare our children and grandchildren the estate taxes, probate court delays, and administering expenses of a will—or who have no great estates to leave in any event—should look into the matter of "living" trusts, or trusts *inter vivos*, to give them their technical name. These are trusts we can set up at any time, and for a specific purpose if we wish, such as a grandchild's college education.

A living trust can be revocable, meaning that we can cancel or alter it. Or it can be irrevocable, meaning that it is fixed as we have designed and signed it. Both forms save administrative expenses, which for a small estate, say $10,000 to $20,000, may come to as much as 20 percent. A revocable trust is subject to the same taxes as a testamentary trust, but an irrevocable trust is not considered part of one's estate and is therefore exempt. So the thriftiest course is to make up one's mind on what to put aside for a grandchild's future and on what terms, and stick to the decision.

A trust necessarily implies a trustee, and that is a most personal choice. A grandchild's parent may be the obvious person to designate, if it is one on whose judgment and sophistication in money matters, no less than his or her love for the child and devotion to the child's interest, we feel we can rely. Banks have trust officers, and there are other trustee institutions. We can make joint trusteeships of an individual and a financial institution in the same way that we can name joint executors of a will, and this may be wise if the investment of large sums is involved. With a living trust we can check on how the business is being managed and satisfy ourselves of the prudence of our trustees.

Savings banks open trustee accounts in one's own or another adult's name for the benefit of minor children, without any special trust document having to be written, and the adult then has control of the account. Different states have different laws under which gifts other than savings bank accounts can be made to minors, and it is best to investigate your state's laws on the subject before committing yourself to one or another form. I am advised that it is quite proper to set up a trust in another state whose laws may better suit your purpose. The giver can be the custodian of the gift, but then the gift is subject to the estate tax. So in this instance the thriftiest course—although not necessarily the preferred one—is to make some other person the custodian of a gift to a child, someone on whose judgment and objective concern you feel you can rely.

Making sure that the right things among your possessions go to the right child or grandchild is also most simply taken care of in a will. But then the objects must go through probate and be subject to the expenses of appraisal, administration, and estate taxation, and if the possessions have intrinsic value this can come to a sizable amount. Art and art objects, antiques, furs, jewelry all come under this heading.

Owners of great art collections give them to museums and yet are able to continue enjoying them during their lifetime, and we are privileged to do the same with our smaller and more personal gifts. All we need to do is to write out a declaration of trust in correct legal form stating that we are holding the object or objects in trust for a particular individual whom we name, and listing the objects we intend for that person. If there are several persons, we make a separate declaration for each. In these arrangements the giver keeps the gift, and the simplest way to convey it to whoever is to have it is by naming the recipient also as the successor trustee. Then all the designated child or grandchild has to do is to take it.

All of us are familiar with and some of us have experienced what can happen to a beloved relative's possessions when no specific arrangements have been made for their distribution. To my mind there is a great deal of comfort in making these decisions and carrying them out in the proper forms ourselves. As for the forms and their uses, lawyers and bank officers can instruct us. There is also a widely popular book, *How to Avoid Probate*, which gives samples of a number of forms and explains their advantages and disadvantages. Another good source of information is *Sylvia Porter's Money Book*, the latest of this well-known columnist's publications, in which she has a chapter on gifts and trusts.

For mature, thoughtful grandparents, finding out what we need to know is no great difficulty, and making wise decisions on what to do with our property and how to do it can be an interesting exercise—as well as a gratifying one. In terms of the eventual joys and benefits to our grandchildren, performing this task is surely an act of love.

In the Rain

My grandmother . . . held that "it is a pity to shut oneself indoors in the country," and used to carry on endless discussions with my father on the very wettest days, because he would send me up to my room with a book instead of letting me stay out of doors. "That is not the way to make him strong and active," she would say sadly, "especially this little man, who needs all the strength and character he can get." . . . In all weathers, even when the rain was coming down in torrents and Françoise had rushed indoors with the precious wicker armchairs, so that they should not get soaked, you would see my grandmother pacing the deserted garden lashed by the storm, pushing back her grey hair in disorder so that her brows might be more free to imbibe the life-giving draughts of wind and rain. She would say, "At last one can breathe!" and would run up and down the soaking paths—too straight and symmetrical for her liking, owing to the want of any feeling for nature in the new gardener—with her keen, jerky little step regulated by the various effects wrought upon her soul by the intoxication of the storm, the force of hygiene, the stupidity of my education and of symmetry in gardens, rather than by any anxiety (for that was quite unknown to her) to save her plum-colored skirt from the spots of mud under which it would gradually disappear.

—*Swann's Way*, by Marcel Proust

10

Advice, Giving Of

Some grandmothers protest that they never give advice, even when asked. Why bother? they say. It's never followed anyway.

One grandmother's comment on that was, Bosh, of course they give advice, and they don't wait until they're asked. We all do it.

She herself took the issue head-on, the day she held her first grandchild in her arms. She said, looking the parents straight in the eye over the sleeping infant's head, "It's no use kidding you or myself. I'm going to be telling you what to do and what not to do, every day of this baby's life. But you don't have to listen."

Times change, methods of child-rearing change, but grandmothers do not change very much where the child's health and happiness seem to be at stake. Turn the calendar back a bit. Your mother-in-law may have held her peace, although you could see her back stiffen. Your mother was probably not so stoic. If you put the baby in its crib, turned off the light, and went out shutting the door, your mother may have said, "In the dark? And with the door closed?" When you put the three-year-old's food down before him and left him to shift for himself, she may have asked, "Shouldn't I help him a little?" If you remained firm in your pre-Spock faith, the first time Grandma babysat she probably confessed, "I rocked the baby—he wouldn't go to sleep for me." And later you caught her surreptitiously ladling food into the toddler's mouth, crooning, "Eat your supper, darling, it's such a good supper."

And now here you are, in the same spot.

How do you feel, when you see your newborn grandchild, perhaps your first, being fed cold milk straight out of the container, not only uncooked but unheated, and in unsterilized bottles? When the young parents' kitchen has not only no sterilizing kettle but not even a bottle brush, and no baby scale in the baby's room, and no stand-up baby bath but a plastic dishpan, in which the precious mite is after all bathed only now and then instead of ritually every day? Do you feel the little hairs stand up on the back of your neck, as I do, when you see the tiny bundle being picked up without a hand at the back of his neck to keep the little head from wobbling?

Yet it is all pediatrically approved—the infrequent weighing, the optional bathing, the casualness about milk and bottles and sterilization and handling. If you were the kind of mother who wore a surgical mask when she prepared the formula (and maybe even sterilized gloves), scrubbed all the crib and bathtub toys (or maybe boiled them), and rigidly observed all the rules about feeding time, bath time, bedtime, you feel very odd indeed at the new scene. All the special care and its inevitable paraphernalia is cut to a minimum. The little darling is taken out of doors not in a big padded behemoth of a baby carriage but in a little gimcracky collapsible thing of canvas and chromium pipestems. Or it is packed into a pouch on a parent's belly, and a few months later stuffed into a pack on a parent's back. This baby seems to be fed not so much on demand as at its parents' convenience; bath time and bedtime appear to follow the same criterion. And yet the new babies thrive and flourish, bright and active.

However strange it all seems, there is one old-fashioned bit of baby-care magic that you possess and the new parents do not, and if it is their first baby and you come to visit soon after it arrives at home you are bound to enjoy one small triumph—you can quiet the crying, fussing morsel. There is something about assured, grandmotherly arms that is instantly transmitted to that knowing little body. The nervous new parents will look at you as though you have performed an instant miracle—what's your secret? they ask. Preen yourself while you can. They will discover soon enough that it is only the confidence of experience.

As for the rest, a grandmother confronted with the new ways of baby and child care swallows her protests and suppresses her shudders. The precious tidbit survives, and so will Grandma, although the chances are that Grandma, at least, will never get used to it.

Some of the young parents abandon the baby foods and the separate baby mealtimes as soon as possible, on the grounds that the child must learn to eat what they eat and when they eat and he may as well begin. Some ignore bedtime, and let the baby and the toddler stay up with the grown-ups and fall asleep on the sofa or the floor, with the same rationale. Rather than pay a babysitter, they take the baby along on evening visits with their friends. At a party the hostess' bed is criss-crossed with young sleepers.

By nursery school or kindergarten age the parents generally institute a regular bedtime. School is school, after all, and children must be delivered to the school doors on time. Most parents recognize the need for a proper breakfast, too, before getting the child off to school. It is only with their last-minute-out-of-bed teen-agers that they begin to have chronic breakfast problems.

All's Well . . .

How do we deal with this turnabout in baby and preschool care? This seems to be a case of every grandmother for herself. If we remember our struggles with our children's grandmother, we generally keep our lips sealed and our hands in our pockets. We may even express admiration for the new methods—heroically, because we are usually quivering like jelly inside, unconvinced that these revolutionary ways can really be good for our precious grandchild.

There is a question I have asked of many grandmothers and I ask it here: No matter what your doubts were at the time, have you ever felt afterward that your grandchild's parents made a serious mistake in their methods of early child care?

Grandmothers whose youngsters have turned out healthy and reasonably happy are bound to answer No, no serious mistakes. And if a physical or emotional difficulty does develop, we are still not able to put a finger on a single cause, because there is usually an accident of birth or constitutional endowment or the difficulty is too complex to be ascribed to a single error.

Apparently most children who are not downright neglected are bound to grow well, whatever method we adopt in feeding, bedtimes, and the rest. Whether or not they follow the rules we followed, most of our young parents know the essentials of a balanced diet, the basic sleep needs of children, the common sense ways of keeping a child well, the normal checkups and shots and when to call the doctor if symptoms appear.

We are learning to pay due respect to individual differences. On countless records an unsuccessful child has been raised by the same parents and with the same methods as other children in the family who have developed normally. An environment that is wholesome for one child may not be ideal for another, and good parents are not necessarily equally good for all their children.

Children draw their genetic endowments not from parents and grandparents alone, but from a vast ancestral pool, and there are mysteries of inborn differences that we may never be able to fathom. It is a bold grandmother indeed who sits in judgment on the parents of her grandchildren, except in gross instances of neglect or cruelty, and when the situation is that obvious, nobody needs to tell her that it is justifiable to intervene.

In the ordinary situation the current fashion in grandmotherly behavior does not call for hovering and criticizing. Many of us are thankful to be too busy to hover, and many of us live too far away for the day-to-day intimacy that would make us experts on a child's individual needs.

Which is not to say that we cannot give an opinion when asked. Obviously we want to be helpful to parents who are trying to do their best for a child.

And when we are asked? Why then we reach down into our memory's store of experience, temper it with what we have observed of the individual child (because one thing is sure, no two children are identical, not even identical twins) and give the most considered opinion in our power—an opinion, I hope, untinged with criticism. By the time we are grandmothers we have learned that most parents, whatever their shortcomings, really try their best. We weren't all that perfect as parents either, as well we realize.

This Dangerous World

Some of the hazards of our grandchildren's world can keep us up half the night. In the big, uneasy cities even going to school is in our eyes a dangerous undertaking, and playing in the street seems positively lethal. There is a grandmother, I was told, who flies out into the street and stops traffic when her grandson goes out to ride his bicycle. Her son and daughter-in-law live in a dead-end street, and the neighborhood is residential and full of children. But she cannot control her terror of an automobile accident, no matter how much she annoys the neighbors and embarrasses the boy's parents.

Yet, as the children's parents repeatedly tell us, this is the world the children must live in, and they had better learn. There are few parents who do not take basic precautions, and teach the children the essential safety rules.

We have been down this nervous road as mothers, although not perhaps to the same degree. I remember riding with my young daughter on the top of a Fifth Avenue bus, in the days when we still had double-deckers, and nearly jumping out of my skin when my daughter pointed and said, "Look, there's Danny!" And there he was indeed, my twelve-year-old son with his friend, riding their bicycles in a swarm of traffic, calmly keeping to their lane, stopping for the lights, putting out their hands to make the turn. I had not been asked whether they could ride uptown, and if I had I would probably have said an emphatic No. But as I watched the two boys managing so well, I made a pact with myself: no more anxious hours about bikes. (Of course we have it all to go through again when they begin to drive.)

No doubt the world we grew up in seemed dangerous to our parents, as our children's world seemed dangerous to us. Our grandchildren's world is indeed dangerous. On that the accident and crime statistics bear us out. But we cannot ask their parents to lock them up, or bring them up under glass.

Indeed the more sheltered the child, the more vulnerable he is. A child must discover his world, must learn to look after himself. He needs a few sound rules from his parents, to which we can sometimes contribute out of our own experience. But we do not help by injecting our grandmotherly fears, which may be exaggerated, into a situation already anxious enough for parents and perhaps also for a timid, easily frightened child. A panicky child is no better equipped to protect himself than a reckless one, or an uninformed, unprepared one. We are most helpful when we inspire the youngster with confidence built on good information and wise counsel.

So, with our fingers crossed and some convenient wood to touch, we acknowledge that our grandchildren's parents are probably right again in the way they send the children out into the world, as they were when the children were small and safe at home.

They Leave Home

When they go away to college they face a whole new set of challenges, some old, some alarmingly new on the campuses of today, where all the parietal rules have been swept away. It seemed to me even when my daughter went off for her freshman year that a sheltered seventeen-year-old was insufficiently protected by the rules, and too suddenly exposed to the experiments of her more adventurous peers. If the undergraduate life seemed too open then, it is vastly more so today, in the aftermath of the rebellious 1960s.

When Jeanie's parents delivered her to college at the beginning of her freshman year not long ago, they found that her roommate's boyfriend was also sharing the room. To some girls this situation might pose no problem worse than inconvenience. But Jeanie was a home-loving, unsophisticated seventeen-year-old—there are still some!—and largely a stranger to the current sexual scene. Her parents offered to go to the dean and arrange matters, but Jeanie begged to be allowed to handle the situation, and they left her to do it, although uneasily, and went home.

Jeanie's grandmother was appalled. How could they leave this gentle child to deal with such an invasion of her privacy, to say nothing of the sexual spectacle itself? Grandmother was all for driving straight up to the college and extricating Jeanie. The parents counselled patience, although they were scarcely less anxious and were on the telephone with Jeanie every night. Three weeks went by, weeks of heroic self-restraint for grandmother, and then Jeanie reported that she had gone to the dean. She had tried to reason with the roommate first, and had received a rude and bruising retort. Even then she did not complain to the dean about the girl's behavior, but simply asked to have her room changed because she and her roommate did not get along.

So grandmother acknowledged that Jeanie's parents were justified in their confidence that she could deal with the problem, that indeed they had had no choice but to leave it to her to handle, since she had so firmly declined their offer of help. And she had handled it.

Next came a letter to grandmother from Jeanie. Everything was marvelous, her new roommate was a darling, they were getting along superlatively together. And the letter went on to say that the new roommate also had a boyfriend, but he came up only weekends, and not every weekend. And when he was expected, her roommate told her in advance and she moved out and camped with some girls down the hall.

Grandmother could only gape in astonishment. This was, to be sure, a rather more civilized arrangement, but here was Jeanie again inconvenienced, and rather passively accepting the weekend disruptions. Again she was moved to interfere, although on much milder grounds than before. Instead she sat down and did some hard thinking, trying her best to put herself inside her granddaughter's skin. It was still true that with the abolition of most rules grandmother was familiar with, a young person could be thrust into situations and even into sexual adventures for which she might not be ready. On the other hand, the relationship with her peers was also of considerable importance in these years. If Jeanie herself found the occasional inconvenience so easy to accept, it must be because her relationship with her new roommate was rich enough in other compensations. Whatever those might be, the girl was clearly content, and able to accommodate to the boyfriend's visits without resentment.

And so again, we grandmothers find that we must stem our anxieties and learn to have confidence, not only in our grandchildren's parents but in the grandchildren as well.

There is a postscript to Jeanie's story which I cannot resist telling. A friend of the family, who lives in that college town, invited the girl to supper, and in the course of the evening Jeanie told of her adventures with roommates and how they had been resolved. The woman friend asked what Jeanie's parents and grandmother thought of it all. Jeanie couldn't say what her parents thought, because they hadn't said, but as for grandmother—"Oh, Grandma wouldn't think anything of it!"

And that's a tribute to grandmotherly open-mindedness that Grandma knows well she hasn't earned.

The Sibling Scene

Interfering between siblings may not be so hazardous as interfering between parents and their children, but it has its dangers. We may come to the rescue of a younger child when the youngster seems to be getting the worst of it, only to have the youngster turn on us. Around the dinner table with her grandchildren, grandmother listens to the older ones teasing the youngest until the youngest is near tears. No longer able to hear it, Grandma says to the little girl, "Tell them all to go to blazes, honey, they're only trying to confuse you." Whereupon the victim retorts, with some heat, "Oh, Grandma, now you're the one that's confusing me!"

Sibling loyalty is no new phenomenon to us. We surely remember that children band together against their elders, and it is the better part of wisdom not to come between them in their battles with each other, no matter how we sympathize with the loser. The youngest in that teasing session may well have been enjoying the situation, however unsettling it was to her, and she may even have seen it as a test that she had to pass to win her older siblings' respect. Grandmother's support was an offer of alliance with the wrong side altogether.

Another dinner scene, and this time one of the boys was so obstreperous that his father sent him to his room until he could behave properly at the table. The boy went, but a few minutes later he slipped in, left a note on his mother's plate, and vanished again. The note said succinctly, "I hate you, Mom and Dad."

Later, when all was calm again, grandmother told Andy how glad she was that he did not include her in his hate letter. Said Andy, "I wanted to put you in, but I didn't know how to spell Grandma."

The grandmother in this story cherishes it as one of her favorites, not because it taught her anything about giving grandmotherly advice—quite the contrary. It taught her that even when she stayed out of the fray, she was part of the enemy world of adults. At least now and then.

By the time a child has learned how to spell Grandma, however, she is usually no longer one of the enemy adults.

A grandmother talking to me one evening suddenly looked at her watch and excused herself, saying that she had to call her grandson. His parents were in Pakistan, where his father had business, and although the boy is in boarding school, "He likes me to phone him—I call him three times a week."

When parents are far away, grandmother's house is home. And when children are away from home, at school or college, they may telephone grandmother instead of their parents when they are out of sorts. A grandson who was a week or so into his freshman year called grandmother to say how great everything was—his room, his roommate, his teachers, his courses, the college, the town were all super.

Three weeks later he called her again. Everything had turned sour, his courses were awful, in fact the whole college was a disaster and he was thinking of transferring. She heard him out, and gave him some calming advice—don't do anything on impulse, see how things are tomorrow, or next week, and talk to your parents before you take any steps at all. They talked of other things, he became progressively more cheerful, and before hanging up he said, "It's so great to have a grandmother to grumble to!"

And, P.S., he did not change colleges.

The Magic Lantern

Alwyn's grandmother sat in the sitting room only when there were guests, or when, by the south window, she held the *Milwaukee Sentinel* or the *Christian Herald* on a level with the ridge of her old-fashioned corset, discovering what went on in the world through her unsuitably small spectacles. Her life, like that of primitive women, revolved about the place where food was prepared. Her thought and even her recollections were accessory to whatever she was doing at the moment; they resembled her habit of whispering to herself, often with vehemence, while she worked. So it was in the kitchen, her broad lap full of pea pods or stockings to be darned, with one eye on a simmering kettle or the bread rising in pans, that she was most likely to satisfy her grandson's curiosity. Sometimes she replied to questions which he was too young to ask with obscure allusions or partial avowals, which, like the rays of a magic lantern, illuminated with disconnected pictures the darkness of many lives—in fact, the darkness of life itself.

—*The Grandmothers, a Family Portrait,*
by Glenway Westcott

II

A Time to Intervene?

Is there a time to intervene in a young family's affairs?

Suppose your grandchild's father, who may be your son or your son-in-law, is struggling to finish his doctoral thesis, and the child's mother, your daughter-in-law or your daughter, is working to buy the groceries, taking care of the baby, and still going to school, still a year or so from her degree. These days it is not at all an unusual state of affairs.

Many grandparents help with money. Some grandmothers help by taking over the daytime baby care if they live nearby. One grandmother was not content with any of these halfway measures. She dreamed up a plan to clean up the whole situation at one stroke with a heroic rescue job in which she would be the heroine. She wrote to her daughter and made her proposal. "Come and live with us," she said. "We'll buy a house with a separate apartment for you and Jim and Jimmy. I'll take care of Jimmy, you can go to college full time and get your degree, and Jim can finish his thesis. . . ."

It was a lifeline and her daughter grasped it. At the end of the semester she and her husband packed their few pieces of furniture in a U-Haul trailer, loaded up baby and belongings and drove to grandmother's house in the big city.

Daughter was not at first surprised to find her parents still living at the old address—it takes time, after all, to buy a new house. But then her mother revealed that they were not going to move. Here was this nice room in the basement, unused, that she could fix up for the young family. And she was not going to be able to take care of Jimmy after all, because she had taken a job—for the first time in years, oddly enough. But that would be all right, wouldn't it? Because they could still manage perfectly well. They had been managing, back there in California.

What had happened to bring about this reversal? Nothing more, it developed, than a change of heart on grandmother's part. She had made her offer on a wave of warmhearted impulse, and no doubt she had made it sincerely enough at the moment. But in the time it took to set her plan in motion she felt less and less heroic, until finally it all became too much for her to carry through, and in the end all she had to give her daughter was a tattered compromise.

This is both a true and a cautionary tale. Few of us have carried our impulses this far, but I am certain we have all made offers of help that we have lived to regret. So we can understand this grandmother's offer, although she would have done better to think it through before she made it, and see just what it would entail in terms of her own life. We can understand her second thoughts, too, although it is harder to understand why she did not pick up the telephone and confess her change of heart to her daughter, before the young people had pulled up roots in anticipation of the new life. Letting matters go that far calls for some deeper explanation.

And of course there is a deeper explanation, one that has to do with the old parent-child relationship. There is a trap that grandmothers, and grandfathers too, find lying in their path time and again. Shouldn't we give the young family a regular allowance, so that Sally won't have to put the children in a day-care center and take a job, and Richard can quit his job and enter that Ph.D. program he has been talking about? But Richard is past thirty, more than ten years out of college, and he has never yet made an effort toward getting an advanced degree. What reasonable justification can there be for taking over a thirty-year-old man's family support so that he can embark on a program he is only talking wistfully about? Suppose he quits in midstream —how will the grandparents feel then? And even if they are generous enough to put no pressure on him to go through with the program, how will he and his wife feel toward the grandparents, having accepted their investment in a course that they have failed to carry out?

Any of us might fall into that trap of reenacting old patterns of dealing with our children when they were still children and living under our roof. Does that grandmother's performance about buying a new house and taking over the baby, and then backing out of the entire plan, remind you, perhaps, of times when you couldn't quite give your child exactly what she wanted, and so you gave her something "just as good" that you hoped would content her? We try to keep our promises to our children, but too often we are tempted into making promises that we cannot keep. The older they are, the more damage an unkept promise can do. The situations that tempt us into offers of help involve a good deal more than a more splendid doll or a new bicycle.

It's a cunningly concealed trap, a booby-trap, in fact. Our children go away to college still children, and for the next several years we know no more about them than what they choose to tell us. They are growing up, falling in and out of love, having affairs or not, forming more and more adult relationships. We may suspect much but we know little or nothing of all that. Then suddenly they are going to work, getting married, having children.

Your child who went away a head-in-the-clouds teen-ager has become a husband and father or a wife and mother, a wage earner, head of a household—in a word, an adult. And you haven't seen it happening, so how can you really, in your heart, believe it?

But we had better believe it. Because if we do not we are bound to be booby-trapped by our old attitudes, and find ourselves in painful conflict with new realities.

That grandmother was surely booby-trapped. What she was doing was playing house with her daughter's real-life situation. Her rescue operation was a fantasy, and she had not actually taken a single step toward making it a reality. The only step she had taken was one that had made her fantasy unrealizable. By getting a job, something she had not done in years, she had cut out the heart of her plan, which was to take over the care of her infant grandson.

On the whole it is probably better to back away from an ill-conceived plan even at the last minute, than to persevere and try to carry it through. To undertake more than we can manage with comfort is to invite disaster. Something will give, sooner or later, and our relationship with the young family is bound to suffer. But surely it is good grandmotherly wisdom to look, not once but several times, before we leap into any form of intervention in our young people's lives, however well meant.

To Save a Grandchild

When a situation seems to be getting clearly out of hand, a grandmother may feel that she must intervene. She may be well aware that she is becoming involved in something beyond her control, starting something she perhaps cannot finish. Yet it is hard to stand by and see a grandchild drowning in trouble, and not dare to put out a hand.

Sick parents, alcoholic parents, parents so deep in their own personality disturbances that the child is neglected or abused, may move a grandmother to take a responsibility and an authority that are not properly hers. This is not an intervention to be lightly undertaken—the situation must indeed be serious.

A grandmother who did intervene told me the story. She had married a man who was brilliantly successful in business but cold and critical at home, and she had divorced him, but not before his personality had had its impact on her daughter. The daughter married a similarly cold, detached man, and had three sons. They lived in another city, but the grandmother visited often to see her grandchildren, and when the eldest boy was sent away to boarding school it was she, not his parents, who visited him frequently there.

She recognized at an early stage that the boy was in deep emotional difficulties. He was violent and destructive, could not concentrate on his school work, and was a problem to the school. She tried to talk to the boy's parents, but encountered only indifference in the father, and open hostility in her daughter, who brutally declared that she couldn't stand the boy, or his brothers, or their father. The suggestion that as the boy's mother she could do with some professional counselling was angrily rejected. Let Eric sink or swim—she couldn't be bothered.

So grandmother elected herself Eric's surrogate mother. She sought professional advice, and when it was clear that a more structured school might be better for the boy, she investigated schools. When she found one that met with her adviser's approval, she registered Eric at the school and took him there herself. Then she went back to her psychiatric counselor to report, and incidentally told him that she was going up to her daughter's home to tell the parents what she had done.

The psychiatrist gave her a piece of advice which I pass on to other grandmothers who may also dare to step into a parental vacuum for a grandchild's sake.

"No, you do not go to tell them, and then stand there and take the flak," he said. "You call your daughter on the telephone, tell her the name of the school where you have placed the boy, give her the name of the headmaster and his telephone number, say a pleasant goodbye—and hang up."

Heroic Granny

For her own sake as well as the child's, a grandmother who undertakes such heroic measures must seek the opinion of qualified people whose judgment will be more objective than her own, as this grandmother was careful to do.

She must also take stock of her own resources. This grandmother has enough income for her own needs and comfort, but not enough to pay the high cost of Eric's new school and his continuing psychiatric care. So she persuaded the boy's grandfather, her divorced husband, to contribute, and she sells a piece out of her collection of antiques from time to time, to pay the rest. But she made sure of her former husband's contribution and of the value of her collection before she took the irrevocable step of removing Eric from his old school and placing him in the new one.

Heroic grandmothers are nothing new. The grandmothers of immigrant families in the past, the grandmothers of ghetto families today—these are often heroic women who are the center and strength of their grandchildren's lives, often of the children's parents as well. This one was different only in that she wore middle class dress and could draw on the kind of help available to the affluent in effecting her grandson's rescue. When I asked her what would become of the two younger boys she looked downcast. "I hope I will be here if they need me," she said. "We must wait and see."

A grown granddaughter told me about her grandmother, a heroic granny in period style. Grandmother came to see her new grandchild, and found her daughter-in-law and the baby living in near-destitution with no money and almost no food in the house. Her son had simply become bored and walked out, leaving his wife and child without support.

Grandmother called on her son at his business office, discovered he was out, and left a message. She made several more attempts to reach him, and when he did not respond she went to the police and had him arrested and thrown into jail. When he was behind bars she went to see him.

"You're going to stay here," she told him, "until you take up your proper responsibilities as a husband and father." And somewhat sheepishly, but certainly in no doubt that his mother would do what she said she would, the erring son went back to his wife and child. And remained.

Yes, he did. Obviously no grave character defect could have been cured by one act of maternal discipline, however stern. But one can imagine a young husband slamming out of the house after a quarrel, and then staying away in an impulsive—and immature—protest against the burden of a family. His mother's police action would have brought him, as she herself might have said, to his senses. Whatever the emotional dynamics of the situation may have been, the infant daughter, now a mother in her own right, assured me that her parents were never again separated, much less divorced, and that her legendary grandmother was now filling a great-grandmother role with as much éclat as ever.

Differentness Begins at Home

It was with real anticipation and relish that you came into the room that held Grandma, and sat down on your little stool and folded your hands around your knees. For pretty soon Grandma would drop some remark—perhaps a very wilful remark—and begin opening up her mind.

Just the same, I used to feel a little sorry for Alice and me then. We were like little plants that managed to maintain a foothold in a crannied wall, or like Arizona birds who must make their nests in a high cactus, not that it isn't prickly but that there is no other safety to be chosen. However interesting it was to live with Grandma, it was not easy.

Grandma Griswold was—well, what her neighbours called "different." Grandma purposed to be different in more ways than one, and, for her, differentness began at home. The amazing thing about Grandma's housekeeping was that, even to the close of the first quarter of the twentieth century, every utensil, every way of doing, was just as purely eighteenth century as Grandma could manage to keep it. She was ninety-six when she died in 1925, and throughout her life—almost a century long—Grandma held back "modern improvements"—you could hear the ironical quotation marks she always spoke into the phrase—from contaminating her home.

—*Grandma Called It Carnal*, by Bertha Damon

12

Opposition Parties

It was vacation time. The grandchildren and their parents had come East and were staying with one set of grandparents, and Grandma Number One had done the correct thing and invited the second set of grandparents to spend the weekend. When the car came in sight, Gran One, who had been watching for her guests, picked the baby up off the grass, took the toddler by the hand, and went to greet them.

Gran Two threw open the car door, flung her arms out in a wide embracing gesture, and exclaimed, "Hello, children, here's Grandma!"

Gran One handed over the children and stepped back, torn between indignation and laughter, realizing that with two words the opposition had rendered her a non-grandmother.

No doubt any of us would feel the same. And no doubt any of us, on the opposition side, would have the same unthinking impulse on greeting our grandchildren, although ordinary civility might curb its utterance in the very presence of the other grandmother. Doesn't every grandmother think of herself as the children's one and only Grandma? And aren't we all inclined to bristle when the rival grandmother shares the scene?

It's bad enough when the children fly in from across the country and both of us are unavoidably on hand to meet them at the airport. "That other grandmother always has a handbag full of lollypops," a friend tells me, "so naturally the children run to her first, and I'm left standing there, seething." Why doesn't she stock up with lollypops too? "Wouldn't think of it," she says. "I love them too much to give them stuff that's bad for their teeth." And that's a classic grandmotherly barb at the competition. That other grandmother doesn't even *love* the children as I do!

The competition is still sharper when both live within easy visiting distance of the children. The better part of wisdom then is to avoid direct confrontation whenever possible. We stagger our visits in order to miss each other, and we tactfully let the children's parents know that there is no need to invite us together. For major events, anniversaries, birthdays, Christmases and such, we can face each other with reasonably good grace provided the party is big enough and doesn't go on too long.

Because there is no blinking the fact that however much we may try to be friends, essentially we are competitors. We watch each other like diplomats from hostile countries. We count each other's gifts, measure each other's contributions to the welfare and happiness of the young family. We are suspicious of every move, critical of every action. The opposition is always doing either too little or too much. And when there is trouble in the young family, we can always find something in the opposition's behavior or attitude to blame.

Friends at Arm's Length

One of my grandmother consultants goes so far as to hold that we should not try to be friends with the opposition party—a polite arm's-length friendliness is the wisest limit. Too much closeness breeds too much shared knowledge, both of each other's doings and of the state of our children's marriage. The less we know, the less we are tempted to criticize, to blame, to interfere.

Suppose there is a preexisting friendship? What if the children of old friends grow up to marry each other? When the children of old friends marry it may seem to the parents that the marriage was made in heaven. But it is a rare friendship that can survive if the marriage turns out, as well it may, to be not heavenly but human and pockmarked with human failings if not with fatal flaws.

The arrival of grandchildren also brings general rejoicing. But the grandchildren add new and potentially explosive ingredients to the volatile mixture, and the friendship of the grandparents is put through a whole new series of tests.

I have a fantasy of how it might be if grandparents, whether or not they were friends before, could become friends after their children marry, and could collaborate in doing what is best for the young family. Young parents, struggling to get on with their professions and give good care to their children, usually with too little money, can do with help from loving sources whether in money or services and preferably in both. Cooperating grandparents could almost recreate the long-lost extended family, spelling each other in giving the hard-pressed young parents a hand. Two grandmothers on the spot ought to be twice as good as one.

Search as I may, I have not found or heard of such a harmonious grandparental duet. If it exists at all it is probably rare, for at least one obvious reason. Too many young families live too far away from either or both grandmothers for any extensive personal service (that does not exclude money, of course, which can go by mail). Still I cherish my vision of a little community of grandparents joining forces in the interests of their children and grandchildren. It would be a beautiful phenomenon, and it is not beyond imagining.

For most of us a son's or a daughter's marriage is the only link between the two sets of grandparents, and it is a slender bond at best. In our mobile society, the most dissimilar backgrounds do not discourage young people from marrying each other, and many of us have seen our child, and eventually our grandchildren, drawn into a way of life that is not to our liking. The other grandparents are too rich, too poor, too conventional, too unconventional, too intellectual, too unintellectual, too conservative, too liberal—in a word, too different from ourselves.

If the differences are sharp enough, it is rather a relief to realize that we don't, after all, have to become *bosom* friends. It is the son-in-law or daughter-in-law who has a claim to our affections, not his or her parents.

At the same time, although we don't have to live in each other's pockets, for the sake of our children and grandchildren we do make an effort. We try to emphasize whatever we have in common. We observe the friendly customs of sending cards, making phone calls, giving and accepting invitations when the children are involved.

And if we are unhappy about possible adverse influences on our child and future grandchildren, it is salutary to recognize that we have had an equal chance with the other parents while our son or daughter was under our own roof. We have transmitted our values to our child, as they have to theirs. From here on, the young couple are in charge of their own lives and the directions they take will be not ours or the other parents' but their own. If you wait it out, says one experienced grandmother, the ingredients you have put into your child will bake out close to your own kind of cake.

As for the grandchildren, like my friend who refused to fight a lollypop war, we can decline to join battle. We create our bonds with our grandchildren on our own ground, by following our own ways and being ourselves.

Our In-Law Children

An astute grandmotherly observer of families pointed out to me that parents who have children only of one sex find it relatively easy to adopt the in-law of the other sex as their own child. My own observation has been that parents who have daughters and no sons sometimes go too far in embracing their sons-in-law. A father who is a successful businessman can hardly wait to take his son-in-law into the business and give him too much too soon—too big a title and too big an income before he has had the experience to earn either. Or he sets the young couple up in a style that they cannot afford and then gives them an allowance to pay for it.

Father-in-law's money seems a foolproof means to provide for daughter's and grandchildren's security, but too often it turns out to be bristling with risk. A son-in-law of independent spirit may refuse to accept his father-in-law's beneficence, and the result may be bitter feelings. Or he can acquiesce, and become an ineffectual drone for whom no one has much use, not even his wife.

A young couple may accept too much help from parents for too long and then feel guilty about it, and their guilt and the inevitable resentment growing out of it poisons the relationship. I have seen marriages go on the rocks under the too assiduous piloting of loving parents-in-law. Perhaps those marriages would have failed anyway, but there is always a chance that the young people might have made a go of it if they had been left to themselves.

Many a widowed grandmother leans on her son-in-law as she might on a son, in ways that are burdensome for the young family and that in the end are not wholesome for her either. All things considered, the in-law relationship seems to be at its best when parents and children each maintain their independence, and build their friendship on mutual esteem and shared interests.

As for daughters-in-law, most of the folk wisdom seems nowadays to be proved only by exceptions to the rule. A mother-in-law is said to be more welcome in her daughter's than her daughter-in-law's house, but the grandmothers I have talked to are in the kitchen with a daughter-in-law more often than with a daughter. A son is supposed to complain that his wife can't cook—"it never tastes like Mom's"—but I know at least one son who tells his mother that her cooking is no match for his wife's. And I know a daughter-in-law who brings her mother-in-law home-baked breads and cakes and home-preserved jams and jellies that mother-in-law, a lifelong professional woman, would never dream of attempting.

Still another reversal of the old rule is what happens when a son isn't getting along with his mother, and daughter-in-law steps in to keep the waters calm between them. More than one daughter-in-law I know has taken over the letter-writing and telephoning, not only to her own parents but to her husband's. Many a grandmother has reason to feel grateful to a daughter-in-law's nurturing of the relationship between the families—and without that good relationship, good grandmothering can become next to impossible. But of course it has to work both ways. The successful grandmothers I know are almost without exception successful mothers-in-law as well.

For one rule I have found no exception. It is a rule I have from a great-grandmother, who says that if a daughter-in-law isn't getting along with her mother-in-law it's because she isn't getting along with her husband. That one has the solid sound of a universal truth.

What we must expect, no doubt, is that the qualities a husband and wife can least tolerate in each other seem to appear in exaggerated form in the spouse's parents. An old man's counsel to a young man on choosing a wife is that he look not at the girl but at her mother (see Ezekiel xvi:44, "As is the mother, so is her daughter"). It may be that today, when the young people choose each other first and meet each other's parents only afterward, it is ourselves and not the prospective spouses who must pass inspection. Our in-law children do not have to win our favor. They can be friends with us or not, as they choose. If we want to be friends with them, it is we who must make the effort.

And the effort must be made, if not for our son's or daughter's sake, then for our grandchildren's, and most of all for our own. Family ties are no longer binding. I know a grandmother who was denied access to her grandchildren altogether, by a son-in-law who felt that his wife's family was his rival in her affections. The ban lasted close to a year, until the wife took a stand. Marriage ties are not much more durable, and our grandchildren can leave us forever in the custody of a daughter-in-law (and more and more often a son-in-law—see Chapter 13) whose bond with us is dissolved with the dissolution of the marriage.

On the positive side, I have run into countless daughters-in-law who do not abandon their ex-husband's parents. A remarkable number of daughters-in-law become attached to a mother-in-law as they have not been attached to their own mothers—for what reason, I leave it to wiser heads than mine to interpret. What I do know is that in all these instances the mother-in-law has put herself out to make friends with her daughter-in-law, and the effort has been rewarded.

In every one of these instances, the mother-in-law has approached her new daughter as a younger equal, a woman in her own right, rather than simply as the wife of her son. Partly, I dare to guess, this has been possible because as mothers we were warned, long ago during the Freudian revolution, that we must not be possessive toward our sons, lest we bring down the curse of the Oedipus complex (somehow the Freudians never did as thorough a job on fathers of daughters with the Electra menace). For another possible reason, many of us have made a full life for ourselves, and we have not needed to attach our sons to us in the traditional way of women without enough scope or satisfactions, whether within or outside the four walls of home. That is the way I see the modern mother-in-law—and the modern grandmother.

The Open-Door Policy

We make the effort, but there is no guarantee of success. The differences in values may be too great, or the chemistry of personalities too incompatible. The in-law child, son-in-law or daughter-in-law, may never be our friend.

Still, as one hardy grandmother pointed out to me, we must never place ourselves in the position of losing our own child—and in consequence, our grandchildren as well. If we cannot be friends with our in-law child, we need not become enemies. Friendliness is still possible even if friendship is not. It is up to us to keep the doors open.

When we feel ourselves rejected it is hard not to be rejecting in turn. But the stakes are really too high. When we turn critical toward our child's spouse, where do we imagine our son's or daughter's loyalty will be fixed? Not on us, we can be sure. And if we are not sure, do we want to drive a wedge into the marriage? What kind of parental love would that be? Furthermore, for a guess, if our son or daughter does divorce, and then marries again, the next spouse may be even less to our liking, and all we have accomplished is a lot of costly mischief. In any event that's a dangerous game to play. Our grown sons and daughters have a right to their own mistakes, as we had a right to ours.

Our course, it seems to me, can only be one of treading lightly around a marriage that gives us no joy. Whether the marriage succeeds or fails, the outcome cannot be of our doing. If the unresponsive (to us) spouse is making our son or daughter happy, we must keep hands off. If not, we must equally keep hands off. It is our child's right to make the decision whether to continue the marriage or break it off.

A prime mistake, as things may turn out, is to alienate the in-law parent of our grandchildren. Whether the marriage survives or falls, we still have our bond with our grandchildren, and it is in our dearest interest to protect that bond.

Over and over I hear stories of grandparents who will have nothing to do with their ex-son-in-law or ex-daughter-in-law. Whatever the actual reasons for the divorce, in their minds the other party is at fault, and they will have none of him or her.

Here is a true case of a divorced father, traveling with his children on a trip to see his own parents. The children's maternal grandmother had broken off relations with him since the divorce, so he could not take them to see her although they had asked to make the visit and she lived in the same city as his parents. But what about great-grandmother, who also lived in that city? The children were asking to see her, too. Did his ex-wife think great-grandmother would receive him?

"But of course!" replied his ex-wife, who knew her old Granny was a far wiser woman than her own mother, "Great-Gran will put out the red carpet for you!" And so she did, marshalling a Sunday brunch of mountains of griddle cakes, French toast, sausages, bacon, sweet rolls, biscuits, jellies and preserves, mostly made by her own hands, the festive delights with which she used to stuff the children's mother as a child. The children had a ball, so did their father, and so did Great-Gran. The only one who was deprived, and by her own doing, was the children's grandmother.

Sooner or later the children want an explanation of grandmother's refusal to see one of their parents. Their mother tells them, "Grandma is still mad at Daddy because of the divorce. I'm not mad at him," she hastens to add in the interest of good feeling, "only Grandma is."

How are the children to interpret this puzzling grandmotherly behavior? And why does grandmother, of all people, perpetuate the hostilities long after the parties who suffered the divorce at first hand have come to terms with each other? A more suitable role for a grandmother is that of peacemaker, for everyone's sake but primarily for the children's.

And they do need us. I remember from somewhere a story of two little boys walking home from school with their arms around each other. One of them was apparently commiserating with the other about his parents' divorce, and the second one said, "Oh, it's not so bad—I'm just divorced from my father, not from my mother."

Whatever the rights and wrongs of a divorce, it is over and done. It has separated husband and wife from each other, but not the children from either. Grandmother's blacklisting of one of their parents is bound to revive unsettling questions in the children's minds, and to exacerbate the painfully divided loyalties that wise parents do their best to allay. No doubt grandmother feels better when she can nurse her anger against her son-in-law. But to show that anger by overt action is an ungrandmotherly self-indulgence.

When we fail to make friends with an in-law child it may be no fault of our own. Apart from the mysteries of personal chemistry, there are emotional forces at work that are beyond our control. Our success depends not only on ourselves, but on the success of the marriage, the successful relationship we have with our grown child, even the kind of relationship our in-law child has with his or her own parents. A daughter-in-law who is too attached to her mother may never be warm to her mother-in-law. Or, if she does not get along with her mother, she may be wary of all mother-daughter relationships.

It is the same, and perhaps more so, with a son-in-law. A man who has had stormy times with his mother is likely to experience difficulties not only with his mother-in-law but with all women, including his wife.

In such situations all we can do is our best. "Be sparing of your nose," is one veteran grandmother's first rule. What she is saying is, Don't poke, don't pry, don't ask for trouble, or you will undoubtedly get it. Stay well away from the storm center. Keep your distance—but keep it friendly.

A Refuge

The candy store was in a non-Jewish part of Brooklyn, and my grandmother ran it all by herself, seven days a week—she couldn't afford to close for the Sabbath, and Sunday was a good business day too, so she never took a day off. She had very bad varicose veins from standing sixteen hours a day, selling candy bars, soft drinks, sodas, and stationery. She looked like a Russian peasant in her mouton coat, with a woolen scarf over her head in the wintertime, and her black lisle stockings and old-lady shoes.

My grandmother was my refuge. No matter how miserable I was at home, I always brightened up with her. I loved going to her house Friday nights for supper. When I was coming she cooked up a storm. She began cooking at six o'clock in the morning—potato pancakes, chicken soup, and boiled chicken. After dinner she would take me into the candy store and make a big malted milk and urge ice cream cones on me. "Julie, aren't you hungry yet?" she would ask me every half hour.

—*My Nights and Days*, by "Julie"

13

Dissension and Divorce

With one out of three marriages in America ending in divorce—in California, one out of two—it is highly probable that one pair of parents of our grandchildren will be among the divorcing couples.

Grandmothers who have been through this experience acknowledge that nothing short of actual tragedy could cause them so much pain. And a large part of the pain, they say, comes from the feeling of helplessness. Divorce is one situation in which they are outsiders whose interference may more often do harm than good.

As far as the divorcing parents are concerned, this is surely true. When dissension between husband and wife arises, no one, and especially not the mother of one of them, has the right to step in. It may happen that one of them—and it may be the in-law rather than our own son or daughter—turns to us with complaints against the other, may even beg us to "do something, please!" And willy-nilly we may find ourselves playing marriage counselor, trying to save the marriage.

This is rarely a successful effort. If we take sides, even if we are invited to help we are no help but a hindrance to any chance of reconciliation. And even if we remain strictly impartial—an unlikely possibility at best—unless both partners to the marriage truly want to save it, no intervention however objective has much chance to effect a reconciliation. The young people may try again out of sheer good will toward us, because we ask it, but usually it is to no avail. When people seriously contemplate divorce the sickness of their marriage is usually too advanced for cure. And how can we be sure that the marriage should be saved?

There is one situation, a strictly contemporary one, in which grandparents may be able to calm the storm and gain a little time for a shaky relationship to reach equilibrium. That is when a wife and mother, most often a young one, becomes restless within the constricted life of caring for small children and is tempted by the greener field of going back to work or to school. She may or may not be realistic about her expectations. Her husband may be as unrealistic, for his part, about the disruption her plans will cause in his home and his children's lives.

Conflicts like these can be sharp and wounding. Discontents that were tolerable now loom larger than life, and a marriage that does not deserve to fail may teeter on the edge of disaster. Here is where grandparents who have the trust of both young people can step in. They can suggest a trial run at work or school, can help to work out a feasible timetable, and a grandmother, if she has the time and the willingness, can perhaps do a spell of babysitting until the new arrangements fall into smooth running order. Many husbands have found a way to accommodate a wife's aspirations, once their reasonableness and their value become evident. And many wives are willing to postpone their plans if, for the time being, they prove too difficult to realize. Sometimes a small beginning can be made, an evening course or a part-time job that can be done at home, until the children are at least of school age.

If it works, then we have accomplished something. If not, we have tried. In either case we must accept the outcome, and if we are wise we will accept it without blame or recrimination against either of the parents. However they manage it, it is their life to manage.

If we cannot play a role in saving the marriage, there is a positive and significant role we can play. We can become the guardians of the children's interests.

Not that the parents are unconcerned for the children. Most parents would claim that the children's welfare comes first with them, and we do not question their sincerity. But human beings are what they are, and bitter and vengeful emotions can override the best intentions. When two people are locked in marital battle, they reach for any weapon to use against each other, and the children are a powerful weapon.

Lawyers, too, are genuinely concerned for the children. So are judges, if the dispute finally comes to be thrashed out in court. But a lawyer is by definition in an adversary position. He can persuade his client, but he cannot act against his client's wishes. And a judge can decide an issue only on the basis of the evidence before him—which, in these intense, complicated battles of personalities, can never be complete.

A judge, furthermore, is also a human being, swayed by his own attitudes and beliefs. Often an award of custody or child support is decided less on the basis of the children's need for one parent rather than the other, but more as a way of punishing the parent whom the judge perceives to be the guilty party, or whom he considers unworthy because of an unconventional living style, or a history of political or religious dissent. In a conservative judge's eyes, any deviation from social institutions that he considers inviolable may disqualify a parent for custody.

There is also a question of money. The parent with greater financial resources can call in the psychologist, the psychiatrist, the private investigator, to help build the case against the other. And this evidence—which may also not be the whole story—is what the court must go on in making decisions that affect the children.

So who is left to keep a wholly objective, wholly devoted eye on the children's welfare? Who but grandmother and grandfather?

And incidentally the pain of a most painful situation is less when we find there is something useful, after all, that we can do.

Children of Divorce

To play this worthwhile role on behalf of our grandchildren we need some solid information about the ins and outs of the divorce process. We need to know what questions to ask the lawyer who is handling our son's or daughter's side of the case.

But first I want to stick a pin in some over-age myths about the effects of divorce on children.

One of these myths is that children out of broken homes are almost inevitably doomed to an unhappy future. Some years ago I was fortunate enough to work on a book called *Children of Divorce* with Dr. J. Louise Despert, one of the leading child psychiatrists in the country and one who had a special gift in dealing with very young children. The book is still in print as I write, and I have been told that lawyers have given it to their clients and judges have read passages aloud from it in court—proof, if any were needed, of Dr. Despert's enduring wisdom.

Her first principle, about which she was emphatic, was that actual divorce is far more wholesome for children than a continuing marriage in which the parents are emotionally divorced. Children can always deal better with a clear reality than with the disturbing confusions of an unresolved situation. Quarreling, bickering, fighting between discontented parents are bad enough. Coldness and indifference are worse.

Her second principle was that divorce does not automatically scar the children. On the contrary, if it is well and lovingly presented to them, and if the resulting change in their lives is considerately managed, they need suffer no lifelong harm.

What usually happens in a well-handled divorce is that the children grow up a little faster. The understanding that they gain of adult needs in their relationships hastens their emotional maturity. Six- and seven-year-olds who have been well guided through their parents' divorce and its aftermath can astonish us with their insights into their parents, their siblings, even themselves.

We cannot count on this maturity. At best it is uneven—they still have only a six- or seven-year-old's experience of life, no matter how wise they may sound. At worst it may be simply a parrotlike echo of what mother or father has told them, a glib cover for what they really feel. And we must expect unhappy episodes, outbursts of anger without apparent cause, sudden tears at what seem to us trivial disappointments. We will see troubling behavior, evidence of anxiety and grief to which the child cannot give words.

For all this we have to be prepared. The breakup of their home and the departure of a parent is hard to accept even when it is explained and apparently understood. They still wish that Mommy and Daddy could be together again and things go on as they did before—or rather, better than before. And don't we cherish the same unrealistic wish?

But it is not an inevitably and irreversibly ruinous experience for children. Human beings are the most adaptable of the earth's species, and children adapt to change more readily and skillfully than most adults. The divorce of their parents is a harsh change, but the children get through it. We can be alert for signs of suffering, but we need not be anxious.

One of the ways we can help them is with the expression, not necessarily in words, of our own confidence that they can survive the change in good order. Apart from their grief at the parting of their parents, children are aware of their dependence, and a lurking anxiety that they cannot express is about their own future. Who will take care of them? For this the presence of a steady, unchanging grandmother is a first-rate antidote, and the stable serenity of grandmother's house is reassurance of the finest quality.

Whose Custody?

The issues of custody, support, and visitation are the ones that directly affect the children. I am told that in 85 percent of divorces these are agreed upon before the court hears the case, along with property division and such practical matters. The two lawyers make offers and counter-offers, the parties arrive at a compromise that both accept, and the court accepts the agreement as part of the divorce decree. Unless there is some gross inequality or some obvious neglect of the children's interest, a judge rarely questions its terms. And when both parties want the divorce they can usually arrive at a fair settlement of the issues between them.

It is when one of them feels aggrieved and vengeful that difficulties arise, or when one of them is so desolated at the prospect of being abandoned as not to pay attention to the details of the agreement, or perhaps not even to care. A wife can be thrown into deep depression by her feelings of rejection and inadequacy, and by a vision of managing her household and children by herself, usually with not enough money. A husband can be in despair at being deprived at a single stroke of home and family.

A grandmother—or grandparents—may well step in at this point, before the agreement is concluded, if only to understand its terms in relation to the children. Grandparents have no rights here but in reality they can be very much involved.

If custody is given to the in-law parent, will they be parted forever from their grandchildren? Or will the visitation rights of the non-custodian parent, their son or daughter, be adequate to include their continuing relationship with the children?

Will the agreed support be adequate? Will their daughter, if she has custody, have to go to work? And if she goes to work, to support herself in the absence of alimony, what provision is there for daytime care of the children? Will the grandparents have to contribute, either financially or with child care?

These are clear and practical concerns for grandparents, and the only way to deal with them is to ask questions and discuss the answers in terms of the children's rights and our own concerns. Grandparents have every reason to go directly to their son's or daughter's lawyer, make it clear that they will pay for his time, and use the time to get the information they want.

The answers they get may still be unsatisfactory. If they ask why their daughter is to get so little financial support, they may be told that that is all their son-in-law can afford, or that is all the court is likely to award in the given circumstances. If they ask why their son has such minimum visitation, they may learn that he feels he cannot keep the children for longer periods, having no one to look after them. Do the grandparents want to take the children for visits as part of their son's visitation rights? Perhaps that can be arranged with the children's mother. And so on and so on.

In the past, custody was rarely an issue. It was granted almost automatically to the mother, unless she was clearly unfit or in the unusual circumstances of her not wanting to keep the children. In the past, fathers were not often confident that they could care for the children, especially young ones. That was traditionally a woman's job. And traditionally a divorced man already had a new wife in prospect, or was looking for one, and was presumed ready to father a new family.

Parental roles have been changing in these years. Fathers are more involved with their young children than they used to be, and with household duties as well. Mothers are more likely to be involved with careers and professions. That a father might ask for custody, even of young children, is no longer so unusual. Sometimes he even gets it, either because the mother does not contest it or because she is judged less fit. She need not be physically or mentally ill, or an alcoholic, or an unworthy mother on certain old-fashioned grounds, although that too has happened in some states. A woman may be judged "immoral" or "abandoned," meaning that she is shown to have had extramarital affairs, or perhaps just one, with the man she plans to marry after her divorce. But a father may be given custody simply because he has an adequate house or apartment, works at home or at adjustable hours, has been cooking and cleaning and caring for the children already. Some fathers nowadays are very good mothers, better than some mothers.

The other side of this issue is less reassuring. Husbands who feel themselves rejected have recently been using these arguments for custody, not because they want the children, but because they want to punish their wives. "I'm going to take your children away from you" is what they are saying, although in lawyerly language.

Here again is where grandparents may well step in. And whether the parent demanding custody is their own or their in-law son or daughter, one hopes that they will consider the question only as one concerning the children's best interest. Grandparents have no legal rights, unless they want to go to court as third parties asking for custody. But if they have tried through the years of the marriage to maintain good relationships with both parents of their grandchildren, they may have some moral weight.

When Grandparents Intervene

Grandparents have intervened in custody cases and sometimes they have won custody of their grandchildren. I read of one case in which they won custody of their seven-year-old grandson away from his father, as a consequence not of divorce but of the death of the boy's mother, their daughter. The marriage had been a happy one, and she had named her husband as the guardian of their son. The widowed husband had a new wife, a woman of good education and unblemished character, who had had experience with children and wanted her stepson to live with her and his father. Yet the grandparents fought the case through the courts, and won.

Why did they want to take the boy away from his father, against their daughter's express wish? They were wealthy, conservative people and no doubt they sincerely believed they could give the boy a better future than his father, who was a mere university teacher. But from the case records it is clear that their deeper reason was their total disapproval of their son-in-law. No matter that he had made their daughter happy while she lived, that she had entrusted him with her son. What they offered in court against him was that he was an agnostic, if not an outright atheist, and a political liberal who had once endangered his job on a university faculty by openly supporting the American Civil Liberties Union. As it happened, the judge agreed with them, and awarded them custody of the boy.

Whether the boy was consulted in this decision, the account does not say, but his preference seems to be implied in what happened later. The father, undiscouraged, persuaded the grandparents to let his son visit him in California, and then refused to send the boy back. At that point the grandparents gave up their claim and the boy remained with his father and stepmother. An odd case altogether, and I for one do not admire the grandparents' role in it, when the father so strongly wished to keep his boy and there was nothing to be said against him except that his religious and political beliefs were at variance with those of his parents-in-law, and had no discernible relevance to his competence as a father.

And here is another case, in which I have only admiration for the husband and his parents in their concern for a very young child. This was a divorce, and the father's parents were given temporary custody of their grandchild while he brought suit for the child's custody. The child's mother had been in a mental hospital twice, for a month each time, and he claimed that she had become addicted to amphetamines, which she had taken to lose weight, and was still addicted. Her lawyer and a court-appointed psychiatrist said he was mistaken.

But with his parents' moral and financial support he brought another psychiatrist into the case and engaged a private investigator who found the pharmacist from whom his wife was still buying the drug. With this evidence the judge gave the mother a rigid program for her rehabilitation, with regular reports (including urine samples) to be made to the court. After a year, he said, if she had followed his orders she could apply again for custody of her child. And so she did, and a year later, cured and well, she regained her child.

This is an example of how a parent and grandparents, together with an enlightened judge and enough money to engage the professional help they needed, were able to protect a child's genuine welfare—and incidentally to reclaim a young woman from a dangerous addiction. Their aim was not to separate the mother from her child but to see her cured of her addiction before the child was entrusted to her. It is no small part of the grandparents' contribution to the outcome that they cared for their granddaughter from the age of one and a half, through the long court proceedings and the year of their daughter-in-law's cure.

A grandmother who is close to her grandchildren may feel strongly that the children's expressed wish to live with one parent rather than the other should be a determining factor in deciding their custody, but it is not necessarily the best guide. Young children hardly ever know what is best for them—they only know what they like. They may say they want to live with Daddy because he gives them pizza for supper and takes them to the movies, while Mommy makes them eat their vegetables and go to bed on time. An older child's preference may be given more weight. But when there is bitterness between parents, an older child may be playing one against the other and it is not easy to discover his real desire, let alone his best interests.

Even a child psychologist with a long list of degrees can be misled by a child's answers to certain stock questions. One such professional, called by the father's lawyer in a custody case, asked a six-year-old, "Are you afraid of your mother?" and the child answered yes, she was. The same child, after a visit to her father, made the unsolicited comment to her mother, "Papa is scary." Pressed, she explained, "I fell down and hurt myself and Papa didn't care." Pressed still further, she admitted that she had climbed where her father had warned her she might fall. When she disobeyed and did indeed fall, this father apparently felt that her bloody knee was her own responsibility. It was his way of teaching her a lesson. A Spartan approach, one feels, but not, in adult terms, frightening. If the psychologist had put the same question about the child's father as she had about the mother, the child would obviously have given the same answer—yes, she was afraid of her father. But those who knew the child and her parents knew that she was really not afraid of either, although she had learned that it was uncomfortable to be as free with her father as she could be with her mother. "You don't answer back to Papa," was the way she put it to her grandmother. Yet even grandmother, who felt no great warmth for her ex-son-in-law, could not say he was not a good father.

Children do not always have the words to say what they mean, and often they seem to speak in a code we cannot decipher. Psychologists, with all their special training, have no Rosetta Stone either. They cannot penetrate the meaning behind the child's answers in one or two meetings, whatever tests they may use. Even when we know the child, we must listen with more than our ears to find the key.

Aftermath

Grandparents may be more involved in the aftermath of a divorce than they have been in the divorce itself. When the child support is indeed inadequate, they can hardly withhold their financial help. But they should remember that the court does hear requests for relief when the terms of the original settlement prove unsatisfactory. Suppose the father's finances have improved, and he would now seem able to contribute more generously to his children's needs. He may, of course, have married again and begun to raise a second family, in which case his improved income is not going to do his first family much good. But if the children's mother is indeed having an unduly hard time, and if the grandparents are burdened, it might be worth at least a lawyer's fee to explore the question.

Grandmothers traditionally become regular babysitters for divorced daughters who must go out to work. We have already mentioned grandmothers who take in the whole family, mother and children, and become surrogate mothers to their grandchildren. This may be a hardship, but it may still be a happier outcome than losing the grandchildren entirely.

Suppose it is your son who divorces, and your daughter-in-law picks up with the children and moves out of your life, breaking off all connection with your grandchildren. This happens more often than anyone but grandparents seem to realize. In one case that I know, the daughter-in-law married again, her new husband offered to adopt the children, and the children's father agreed and signed away his paternal claim to them. The children moved away to a distant home with their new father, who declared his intention of severing all bonds with the family of his wife's first marriage. The grandparents were heartbroken. Their son was embarking on a new life, but they had lost their grandchildren.

Do grandparents have no rights to their grandchildren, and can grandchildren be deprived of their grandparents by a stroke of the pen—and a pen in someone else's hand, to boot? Alas, it is so. The only way that grandparents can keep from losing their grandchildren in these situations is by building and nurturing a friendship with the in-law parent, a friendship that is a direct personal link to that father or mother of the children, and not dependent on their own son or daughter.

We have talked about this before, as a part of general family feeling, and now we see that it can one day become a crucial factor in our lives as grandparents. With the vicissitudes of modern marriage, who knows how firm our son's or daughter's marriage ties may be, how much or little time we may have to build our relationships with our grandchildren? Best to begin right at the beginning, before the grandchildren even come into the world, and make friends with the new son or daughter that has come into the family.

It is possible to keep the grandchildren even with a daughter-in-law who moves away and marries again. When the children's father still cares about them and maintains his visitation rights, we have not lost the children. And not all daughters-in-law turn away from a divorced husband's family. Some daughters-in-law feel closer to their mothers-in-law than to their own mothers, with whom they may never have learned to resolve old conflicts and become friends. Some divorced daughters-in-law continue to be regular visitors—with the children—to their ex-parents-in-law. But this can happen only when a direct friendship has grown between them, one that is more than simply in-law courtesy during the life of the marriage.

In that case of the deprived and grieving grandparents it might have been possible to work out something with the children's adoptive father. The grandparents might well have tried, not at once, but after the family was settled in the new home. They might have written and asked permission to send birthday and Christmas gifts to the grandchildren, perhaps to exchange visits. For this they would of course have had to build on a good relationship with their daughter-in-law during her marriage to their son. They might also have to reassure the children's new father that their attachment to the grandchildren was no threat to his authority as their father. If they had tried, who knows? They might well be seeing the children again. But it would never come about without effort. Grandparents have no legal rights.

Yet when they try, their efforts are not in vain. In one case of a father's early death, his mother, desolated though she was, extended her motherly wing over the widowed daughter-in-law and the children, and created such an enduring bond that when the young widow married again her new husband, too, became part of the family.

In another case it was the daughter who ran away with her lover, abandoning husband and children. This is a new pattern that we are seeing, of women taking their freedom as formerly only men used to do. The son-in-law in this instance was so undone, so helpless to care for his two young children, that the parents of his runaway wife took in the whole family, and grandmother became a mother to his children until he got his bearings. When he took an apartment of his own, he made sure it was near grandmother's, and she continued to watch over the children. When he married again, and settled his wife and the children in a new home, that too was near enough to grandmother's, and the whole family, step-daughter-in-law included, became regular visitors to Grandma's house. If we want to keep our grandchildren, come divorce, come remarriage, it can be done.

I don't know of any book about divorce for grandparents. Who, after all, thinks about grandparents, except other grandparents? I have yet to find, in a magazine or a newspaper, an article on "Grandparents of Divorce." But for those who are in the throes of a son's or a daughter's divorce, and who want to inform themselves on the whole confusing process, I recommend *Uncoupling* by Norman Sheresky, a lawyer with long divorce experience, and Marya Mannes, a distinguished writer and social critic. It is a wise book as well as an informative one, and new enough (1972) to be reliable about the current state of divorce, divorce laws, which differ in every state, and divorce courts and their customs, which differ almost from judge to judge. I have taken most of my stories in this chapter from life, but two are from this book, for which I acknowledge my thanks.

A postscript to this chapter, too late for the first edition of *Grandmothers*, came in two state court decisions which for the first time granted visitation rights to grandparents. In both cases the former daughter-in-law, bitter after her divorce, had severed all links with the grandparents, and one had gone so far as to return, unopened, their birthday and Christmas gifts to the child.

"Animosity between the mother of the children and their grandparents . . . is not a proper yardstick by which to measure the best interests of the children," wrote the New York judges. And the New Jersey court said, "There are benefits which devolve upon the grandchild from the relationship with his grandparents, which he cannot derive from any other relationship. Neither the Legislature nor the court is blind to the human truths which grandparents and grandchildren have always known."

Despite this judicial wisdom, the New York mother was still evading the court order nearly a year later. And in another case a court denied the grandparents' plea on the ground that visits against the custodial parent's wishes were not in the child's best interest.

The law cannot enforce good feelings. So in the end we are left with what we had at the beginning, the opportunity to build such strong bonds with our daughter or son by marriage that our right to see our grandchildren needs no other justification than love.

Elder Victorians

As for the old, though they would try to be amiable to the young, by now crossness had settled in their bones. . . . Moreover, they made their age felt through the medium of many devices. . . . They gloried in their age and the various apparatus of it, and indulged in a wealth of white wigs and fringes, sticks, ebony canes and Bath-chairs, while, as for strokes, these were *de rigueur* from sixty onwards. In fact, it was a generation which, unlike the next one, did not know how to grow young gracefully. . . . Thus, my grandmother Londesborough was seldom now to be seen out of a Bath-chair, although she was still able to exercise her charm on us without effort, and equally to deliver the most portentous snubs when she wished it. . . . Nevertheless, her world had changed —for though she had been train-bearer to Princess Mary of Cambridge, afterwards Duchess of Teck, at Queen Alexandra's wedding to King Edward, and had stayed at Windsor for the ceremony, which took place in St. George's Chapel there, and though, too, she and my grandfather had always belonged to the pleasure-loving, yet she was never Edwardian in the sense that her son and daughter-in-law were. She possessed a stricter outlook, a more severe sense of duty, and all the rather naive, unsophisticated courage of the Victorians, as well as sharing their genuine belief in the conventions.

—*The Scarlet Tree*, by Osbert Sitwell

14

Far Out

There seem to be no limits to the novel situations we grandmothers get into these days, and not of our own doing. These are strange times, and nothing in our girlhood, marriage, or motherhood years, nor in our jobs, professions, or sheer living experience has prepared us for the roles some of us find ourselves playing.

A dream familiar to many is of finding oneself on a theater stage or platform, standing before an audience, knowing that one is expected to speak certain lines or deliver a certain lecture or address, but having no idea what those lines or that speech may be. Grandmothers today are living out that uneasy dream in real life.

Here is a wedding, flower-decked, musical and sedate, the kind of traditional scene that brings tears of joy to most women's eyes and especially to a grandmother's. And here is the grandmother of the bride, tearful and smiling as one would expect. And—surprise, surprise!—in her lap she has a baby, the bride's baby and her own great-grandchild.

Grandmother is holding the baby while its mother is getting married to its father. Beside her stands another of her granddaughters, some five or six months pregnant. This granddaughter is to marry *her* baby's father a month or so from now.

Grandmother remarks, "Isn't it nice when they decide that they want to get married after all!" And that's a line she never learned in her own maiden days, forty or fifty years ago.

Here is a second wedding. No baby is attending its parents' marriage this time. But an old family friend comes up to congratulate the groom's grandmother, and then bends close to her ear to whisper somewhat shamefacedly, "I probably shouldn't repeat this to you, but someone just told me these two young people have been living together—"

And grandmother, not turning a hair, answers, "Well, now, it's no secret. They'd been living together for five years before they agreed to get married. I hope they'll be as happy after they're married as they were before." The old family friend wanders away bemused. That's another speech one never expected to hear from a grandmother.

Know-Nothing Gran

Grandmothers may be meeting these situations with aplomb, but don't let their apparent insouciance fool you. They are not indifferent to the impact of these changes, not unfeeling about the pounding down of social institutions they were reared to believe in. They shudder inwardly, not so much over the tattered proprieties as at the threat to the family, the slackening of mutual responsibility of spouses toward each other and of parents toward children.

They rarely voice these anxieties, and never to the young people. They have schooled themselves not to criticize, not to offer unsought opinions or advice. They say, "If I don't accept the new ways I'll lose my grandchildren," and "We have to keep up with the times, you know, or else we get left behind, and then we're very lonely."

At the same time they confess that it is not all that easy to go along, smiling all the way. Says one, "I'm always happy to have my granddaughter visit, and happy to welcome her boyfriend—but I'm still uncomfortable at having it all go on *under my own roof*!" So she offers them separate rooms, says goodnight, and goes quietly off to bed, closing her eyes and ears and letting them make their own arrangements. And at breakfast she doesn't ask how they have sorted themselves out and they are tactful enough not to raise the subject. They may even believe she doesn't guess, isn't aware of the changing customs of boy and girl.

Grandmother is perfectly willing to let them believe this. She doesn't have to swing with the times if she doesn't want to, and she doesn't have to take a stand that will alienate her young people, even though the new ways make her uncomfortable now and then. She may be keeping her peace but she is not necessarily suffering in silence. On the contrary, she may be having a quietly interesting time, watching to see how the young people come out with their elastic relationships. She has the grandmotherly privilege of affectionate detachment, of loving non-participation. And if the young people believe she doesn't know what's going on, she can enjoy a modest one-upmanship, because she does see and she does know. More often the young people have a sneaking suspicion that Grandma knows much more than she reveals, but they willingly, even gratefully, join in her know-nothing game. It is a fond conspiracy on both sides.

A grandmother of a typically scattered American family lives alone in a southern town, communicating mostly by mail and telephone with sons and daughters in various parts of the country and grown grandchildren who are equally spread about. She is a woman of advanced years, and her standards are old-fashioned and stern—or so her daughters have always believed. One day she has a visit from a granddaughter—call her Helen—who lives in a middle western city. Helen is married and separated from her husband, and is making a vacation trip with a young man with whom she has been living for many months.

Grandmother welcomes them both, looks rather vaguely at the young man as though she thinks he may be the husband, but says nothing. They spend a day driving Grandma around, shopping, seeing the sights of the town and the countryside. They take Grandma out to dinner, then bring her home to her tiny apartment. She offers Helen a bed, apologizes for not having room for them both, but they thank her and explain that they will stay at a motel in order to get an early start in the morning. Helen kisses Grandma, says a loving goodbye and promises that they will come and see her again next year. All three of them have had a genuinely good time together, and for Helen the day has renewed her childhood attachment to her grandmother, as well as adding to it a grown woman's appreciation of Grandma as she is today.

There is more to the story. Helen's mother, and Helen's aunt in a northern city whom she also visits with the boyfriend on this trip, talk on the telephone about Grandma. Is Grandma actually as vague as she seemed? She has been told that Helen is separated from her husband. Did she realize that this young man is Helen's boyfriend? Does she know? Or doesn't she? Helen's aunt had her answer the next time she telephoned to Grandma in the southern town.

"How did you arrange the sleeping when Helen stayed with you?" Grandma asked. "Oh, they slept on that double-bed convertible in the living room," said her daughter. A small chuckle came over the wire, and Grandma said, "Mm, yes, I thought that's how it would be."

So despite her age and her old-fashioned ways, Grandma did know—and did not let on that she knew. Many a grandmother deals with the young people's new ways as this grandmother did, looking a little vague, sounding a little dim, walking softly around issues that it would cause only grief to confront. It is a kind of grandmotherly wisdom to accept what she cannot change, and to hear nothing, see nothing, know nothing—and say nothing. Why speak, when we know that the young people will go on in their own way no matter what we say?

Helen and her boyfriend kept their promise and visited Grandma again on their holiday trip the next year, something they would not have done if Grandma had raised questions about their relationship. Suppose she had abandoned her know-nothing policy. If she acknowledged their arrangement without criticism, she would seem to be giving it her blessing—which, in the light of her lifelong principles, she can not do. If she criticized, they would not change, but they would not be inclined to visit her again. Situated as she is, that would probably mean that she would lose all contact with her granddaughter.

Those are our alternatives. Most of us would feel that to lose our grandchildren is too much of a sacrifice to make for old and now apparently outworn customs.

Some grandmothers have confessed that they feel hypocritical, making up two guest rooms when anyone over the age of five would know that only one is going to be used. I don't care for the word hypocrisy. It is a young people's word, a privileged word of youth which sees only black and white in human behavior, and which is inclined to be self-righteous and quick to sit in judgment. I prefer to invoke the rights of experience, and substitute for hypocrisy a grandmotherly pragmatism.

By the time we are grandmothers, although we have not given up fighting for principle, we are selective about what principles we will fight for. Grandmothers will still lie down in front of bulldozers if they feel strongly about the environment. They will still attend protest meetings, write to their congressmen, and vote their consciences on public issues that seem to them important. But on questions of private behavior, in which not morality but social custom is at issue, they may choose to sit out the battle. They have had enough experience of life to know that the line between right and wrong, good and bad, is not everywhere so sharp as it seemed in youth.

We are old enough to be wary of sitting in judgment on others' behavior. If the young people choose not to institutionalize their relationships, that does not necessarily mean that the relationships are not worthy of respect. An open-minded grandmother, observing from the sidelines, may well come to the conclusion that some of these companionships are more admirable than many marriages. And a patient grandmother often sees them end in marriage. And so we see no need to mount the barricades in defense of old proprieties —especially if it means losing our grandchildren. That is what I call grandmotherly pragmatism.

Add one more situation, the case of the liberated daughter who deliberately and on principle has her baby out of wedlock, and has no intention of marrying the father of her child. We may think this is carrying liberation rather too far. We may believe it is unfair to the father, above all unfair to the child. And we know—as the young mother herself may not fully realize—that she has undertaken a heavy responsibility and a hard way of life. Our society as it is organized today will not give her much if any help. But that is her choice. What do the grandparents of this infant of liberation do?

One grandmother, widowed and alone, resisted the tug as long as she could, and then went to see her grandson. The consequence could have been predicted. She settled down to look after the baby while her daughter went out to earn a living for all three. The situation is exactly the same as that of the divorced young mother. Grandmother takes over the house and baby care while the mother goes to work.

Another pair of grandparents also resisted at first, and then capitulated. They have taken in the child and become in effect its parents while their daughter continues to pursue her adventurous life. For these grandparents, a retired pair who no longer have family, business, or profession around which to organize their lives, the grandchild has become the focus of their happiness. However it came about, the child is a boon to their late years. As for the child, who never knew his father and is unlikely to see much of his mother, the unplanned denouement of the new sexual freedom has provided him with a sheltering home and a full complement of loving, if somewhat elderly, parents.

Terra Incognita

If the new sexual mores have challenged our emotional tolerance in one way, other crossings of old boundary lines have shaken us in other ways. Interfaith marriages are nothing new, although there are more of them than there were in our youth. We hear less than we used to about parents who refuse to recognize the marriage or the grandchildren who are born of it. Still the orthodox of all faiths are required to renounce a son or daughter who marries outside the religion, and I know of a Moslem mother who remained firm in her rejection of her son's marriage and would not see him, his wife, or her grandchildren.

In the standard situation it is the grandfather who is resistant, and the grandmother who refuses to give up her son or daughter. When grandchildren are born, grandmother usually persuades her husband to relent and enjoy the pleasures of grandparenthood with her. And we all know grandparents who accept not only the marriage and the grandchildren but the entire in-law family, and the grandchildren become part of a large clan of varied background and religion. Lucky the grandchildren, and happy the grandparents who can welcome so much diversity within their family embrace.

Marriages that cross ethnic boundaries are also nothing new in a country of immigrants like our own. And now we are experiencing the crossing of racial boundaries.

No one is entitled to minimize the pain of these situations. But it seems to me that there is an area where all faiths and races meet. I think of the passage in the New Testament, in Paul's Epistle to the Corinthians, describing love which suffers all things and forgives all things. If there is any human love that is unconditional, without strings attached, it must be the love of grandparents for grandchildren. And in these situations that grandmothers confront more and more often in our changing world, their love does indeed endure and overcome. Grandmothers—and grandfathers—who have dealt with these situations have told me that the prospect of losing their son or daughter and being alienated from future grandchildren was far more painful than accepting a marriage across boundaries that they used to believe were impassable.

Then there is another terra incognita of the emotions, the acceptance of an adopted child, especially one of another color or culture. Some white families have adopted black children who needed parents. Two wars fought in Asia, the Korean and the Vietnam wars, have resulted in Eurasian children who also have a claim on American families.

When a husband and wife decide to take parental responsibility for a child of another race, how can grandparents do less than accept the child as their grandchild? I must hope that they do. Few grandmothers, in any case, can resist the appeal of a child in need of love, whatever the color of its skin or the shape of its eyes.

And now comes the challenge of a child born of artificial insemination. It is still not a widespread solution for childlessness, and it may never become one, but it occurs. I am told of one such situation, in which the grandmother had no difficulty about embracing her grandchild, but the grandfather did. His son had been infertile, and the grandfather's argument was that the child his daughter-in-law bore was no grandchild of his.

Blood and kinship are concepts reaching back into antiquity. We have only to read the Bible to understand their commanding power over our ancestors. Even today, we scan our grandchildren's faces to see the resemblances to our son or daughter, to aunts and uncles and cousins, to ourselves and our parents and our remembered grandparents. We see character traits both good and bad—"She has the family musical talent," or "He's just like Uncle Harry—he'll come to no good."

With an adopted child, or a child of artificial insemination, we are asked to abandon the ancient blood and kinship attachments. We are asked to accept the child as what he or she is.

It seems to me that this may be a good lesson to us all, one that we may well apply to our grandchildren of our own kith and kin, descended directly from ourselves.

When we hold our new grandchild in our arms for the first time, and examine the little face and body for resemblances to our own children at this infant age, and especially to the child who is this one's parent, we tend to dwell on the resemblances. We tend to forget the enormous mystery of this individual child's genetic endowment, the particular selection of genes from a vast and diverse inheritance that this child, and this child alone, brings into the world. We dwell on the resemblances and ignore the differences. We underestimate the peculiar blend of likeness and unlikeness that makes each human child unique.

When the child develops in familiar ways we say, with the joy of recognition, Yes, this is the way his father, my son, developed. And if some unfamiliar trait appears we say, That must be from his mother, from the other side of the family.

But that's too easy. Because this mystery of a new personality must give one to think. Any of its traits, familiar or unfamiliar, may come from some ancestor of far away and long ago. Or some blend of genes may have created in this child a personality that cannot be traced to any member of either family. A gift for music, a love of machines or snakes or words, a stubborn will or a fierce temper or a fear of heights or a timidity in fights could come from anywhere or nowhere.

Or is it a learned pattern rather than an inherited one? We puzzle over nature versus nurture, we search through inheritance and environment for clues, and most often the clues are inadequate or downright misleading. We may never know what aspects of a child's environment lead to the development of what genetic endowment, because no given environment can ever bring out all of an individual's potential. Except for some outstanding gift that crops up in generation after generation, or a physical characteristic that comes with certain dominant or sex-linked genes, like color blindness, most of what makes up a personality is unique to the particular individual.

When we contemplate how little we can know and how much must remain unknown, even in a child of our own kin, our reliance on kinship and family lines must be shaken at the start. Whether the child is of our own or another family, another culture, or another race, every child is a new creation, mysterious, unique, and a stranger, until we make friends and come to know the small new person.

This Astonishing Old Age

July 5th, 1868: Today I have completed sixty-four Springtimes... And now here I am, a very old woman, embarked on my sixty-fifth year. By one of those strange oddities in my destiny, I am now in much better health, much stronger, much more active, that I ever was in my youth.... I am troubled by no hankering after the days of my youth: I am no longer ambitious for fame: I desire no money except insofar as I should like to be able to leave something to my children and grandchildren.... This astonishing old age... has brought me neither infirmity nor lowered vitality.

Can I still make myself useful? That one may legitimately ask, and I think that I can answer 'yes.' I feel that I may be useful in a more personal, more direct way than ever before. I have, though how I do not know, acquired much wisdom. I am better equipped to bring up children.... It is quite wrong to think of old age as a downward slope. One climbs higher and higher with the advancing years, and that, too, with surprising strides.

How good life is when all that one loves is aswarm with life!

—Letter from George Sand to a friend, quoted in *Lélia, the Life of George Sand*, by André Maurois

15

Are Grandparents Necessary?

With all that we have said about grandmothering and its uses, we may yet have our doubts. Are grandmothers really necessary? In our grown children's and grandchildren's world, in which new ways so often baffle us and old ways seem so readily discarded, is there anything of value left for us to do? Or are we clinging to old sentimentalities and threadbare illusions?

When doubts like these arise, a sensible course is to hear the case for grandmothers from voices more objective than those of our loving families.

William V. Shannon, a member of the *New York Times* editorial board who occasionally writes a column of thoughtful social comment, recently headed one of his columns with the title, "Our Lost Children." In it he talks about the downward trends in reading scores and scholastic aptitude tests, the alarming upward swings of the number of dropouts and of other, far graver signs of distress occurring at younger and younger ages. He observes that in a society growing ever richer in material goods, its children are becoming ever poorer in the emotional and intellectual nurturing that families once gave them.

He is too knowledgeable to ascribe these complex effects to a single cause. But he speaks of the increasing numbers of working mothers, of single-parent families, and—most significantly for us—of the loss of adults other than the parents from the household. He adds, "In a small child's life, 'Captain Kangaroo' is no substitute for a loving grandmother."

Much of what Mr. Shannon says in brief is spelled out in landmark studies on the child in our society by Professor Urie Bronfenbrenner, whose field at Cornell University is family studies. Dr. Bronfenbrenner does not allow us the comfort of believing that only disadvantaged families are failing their children. He tells us that single parents, working mothers, children born out of wedlock, the loss of other adults from the home are patterns now more and more pervasive in middle class family life.

What this says to me is that in these times of swift and sudden change our grandchildren need us more than ever. They need whatever we can give them of ourselves, even if only occasionally and from a distance, and even if they are well provided with loving and dependable parents. If theirs is among the many families in which both parents go out to work, or the one out of three families struck by divorce, or the relatively stable families in which parents nevertheless feel, however subtly, the destructive tides pressing against the nuclear family today, then we should have no doubts of our usefulness. Then our contribution of dependable love and serenity is of immeasurable value to the children, as it may indeed be to the beleaguered parents.

Finally comes Dr. T. Berry Brazelton, the Boston pediatrician, Harvard Medical School professor and author of two books on baby and toddler care. (If the parents of your young grandchildren do not have them, they are an interesting grandmotherly gift: *Infants and Mothers*, and *Toddlers and Parents*. Look at them yourself and see.)

This good doctor cares about new babies' mothers almost as much as he cares about the babies, whom he loves wholeheartedly. And he speaks sadly of the fact that grandmother is now so rarely around to give the calm reassurance that new parents need.

He describes how grandmother, after her visit to help with the new baby, goes home with a feeling of defeat. What has she done to help? But he asserts that she has helped. Her calm presence has helped. Her assured handling of the baby has helped, even though its mother or father has watched her suspiciously, perhaps jealously. She has helped with the soft suggestion that it might be all right to wait a while before calling the doctor, when the inexperienced parent is sure that "something is wrong." And, says Dr. Brazelton, she helps just by being someone for the anxious mother or father to be angry at.

That's a kind of help that I'll bet most of us have never thought of! Did you ever poultice your bruised feelings with the knowledge that you were a valuable, indeed an essential safety valve for your grandchild's parent? The next time you find yourself taking the flak from a grown child or child-in-law, remember Dr. Brazelton and be comforted. Whom else can they safely explode to, without fear of the consequences, if not to us? Who else will stand and absorb it, temper, rudeness, harsh words and all, often without a retort, and never hold it against them? And if the end result is that they can turn back to our grandchild relieved and under control, then who are we to complain? Our bruises melt away like snow under the sun.

And Grandfathers

Grandfathers are joining in this nurturing role. The capacity for loving and giving to a child is as much a part of men's as of women's nature. For generations, men have been discouraged from using this part of themselves—it was an unforgivable kind of discrimination that labeled it the "maternal instinct." Whether or not it is an instinct may be open to question, but surely it is not maternal. It is simply human. We have the evidence of ten thousand generations of human beings for that—and considering the long years of growing and developing during which human children need to be cared for, the species probably would not have survived without it.

A newspaper clipping tells the story of a set of quadruplets who were born to a New Jersey couple not long ago, and how the babies' coming has changed everyone's life, especially the life of the grandparents. These grandparents live nearby, and they have been coming over every day to help. That's a routine task for a grandmother. But here is grandfather also on the job, doing his share of bathing, diapering, feeding, cuddling the babies, and enjoying it so much that he is considering making an early retirement from his law practice to have more time for his grandchildren. He had never done any of these things before—as a young father he had never picked up his own daughter until she was a year old. Fathers of a generation ago were not expected to handle babies, and indeed they were afraid to try. But this grandfather quickly developed both expertise and confidence.

More and more grandmothers are finding that grandfather will cheerfully join them on their grandmotherly errands. In a children's clothing department one is accustomed to seeing mostly mothers and some grandmothers. But on a recent shopping trip for my own youngsters, hearing a man's voice behind me, I turned to see a grandfather holding up a little girl's frilly, flowery nightgown.

"This ought to be her size," he was saying to Grandma beside him, "and I bet she'll like it." Grandma agreed,

Grandpa added it to an armload of granddaughter clothes, and when last I saw them they were disappearing into the boys' department to do the same for their grandson.

Other People's Grandchildren

Grandparents are so necessary to children—and children to grandparents—that Congress passed a law some ten years ago to bring them together. The Foster Grandparent program, first enacted in 1965 and now part of ACTION, the federal agency for volunteer programs, has survived while many other programs to improve people's lives have perished because of underfunding or overexpectations or both.

At the beginning of 1975, between twelve and thirteen thousand men and women in their sixties and older were bringing grandparent love and comfort to children in hospitals, institutions, day-care centers, sometimes in private homes, in 158 projects in all fifty states as well as Puerto Rico, the Virgin Islands, and the District of Columbia.

Each of these grandparents is given two "grandchildren," with each of whom they spend two hours every weekday. They feed and dress the little ones, play games, tell stories, read and teach crafts, help in giving physical and speech therapy to handicapped or retarded youngsters, or just cuddle and talk and listen.

This is an Older Americans program, for which participants qualify by age, good health, and incomes below certain levels, and they receive financial assistance and certain other benefits as well as training for the tasks to which they are assigned. It has been a lifesaver for lonely men and women with no families of their own to help. And it has tapped a precious resource of nurturing affection for children who need it.

Hospitals, institutions, and community projects for children can use such a resource, and grandmothers and grandfathers who have time for grandchildren and none of their own might well look about for what they can do in their own town. Early in these pages I spoke up rather boldly and said that no grandmother who has her health, and who does not have to work for a living, need sit around with time on her hands. I now put the same challenge to grandfathers, especially those who have retired from business or profession and find themselves with more leisure than they can enjoy. If your own grandchildren don't need you all that much, there are other people's grandchildren who do. And if there is no center for volunteer grandparents in your community, it might be a rather good use of that extra leisure to set about organizing one.

A Fair Exchange

Whatever we may have expected of our children, when it comes to our grandchildren we most often give our love freely, without expectation of any return. But for the enhancements we bring to their lives, the many little windows we open for them without really knowing that we do, our grandchildren repay us. Children who are loved know how to give love in return. It seems to me that they give back to us, in a childlike version, the very quality of love that we give to them, that their behavior to us is a diminutive mirror image of ours to them.

Just as we try to show them our kindest, warmest, happiest selves, so when they are alone with us they try to offer us their nicest manners, their pleasantest ways. They praise our skills, accommodate to our oddities, excuse our shortcomings —and as they get older they even enjoy our eccentricities. Indeed our grandchildren accept us for ourselves, without rebuke or criticism or efforts to change us, as no one in our entire lives has ever done, not our parents, siblings, spouse, friends—and hardly ever our grown children.

Our grandchildren try hardest for us, and when we are in charge they are embarrassed if one of them gets out of control. The seven-year-old explains the crying spell of the not-quite-five to Grandma, "He's still pretty babyish but he'll get over it—when he starts going to school and making friends he'll see how nice it is to be grown up." The younger one apologizes for the older one's burst of anger, "She gets mad when I take her things—but sometimes she lends them to me."

They even defend us from our own grown children—as when granddaughter, aged eight, takes Grandma's hand and leads her out of the eye of a daughterly storm into the next room, saying, "Don't worry, Grandma, Mommy's just upset —you know she loves you."

So it is in every way a fair exchange and better than fair.

We pass on to them—we cannot help passing on to them —our values and beliefs, and like little sponges they absorb them. Not that they do not question them later, but in the very questioning they acknowledge the importance of what they have learned from us. A grandmother of long experience told me a story about her own grandfather, one that she has never forgotten and has passed on to her grandchildren. It's the story of the two-cent stamp.

She may have been eight or nine years old when, one day, bringing her grandfather his mail, she noticed that a stamp on one of his letters—a two-cent stamp, so you know how long ago that was—had not been cancelled.

She said gleefully, "Look, Grandpa, here's a stamp you can use again!"

But he said, "No, child, this stamp has done what it was paid to do. It has brought us this letter." And he tore up the envelope, stamp and all, and put it into his wastebasket.

The two-cent stamp story, of old-fashioned honesty and respect for the law, is one that I mean to remember to tell my grandchildren. And I think they'll remember it, too, and pass it on.

Sometimes we feel we do too much for them, sometimes nowhere near enough, but it evens out. For whatever we do, although we ask no reward, we are rewarded. There is no way to measure the diverse gifts with which our grandchildren enrich our lives, simply by their being.

Not the least of these is the enchantment of watching them unfold and flower into new phases of growth, each child following the immutable human pattern, yet each one in his or her unique way. As parents we could never stand back and watch this in our own children with such rapt fascination. We were too close, too involved. As grandparents, however close and involved we may be, we still have that precious modicum of detachment that comes with being the older generation. We are already standing back a step, and we have the perspective from which to watch the seeds of character yielding up their secrets.

I quote again from a grandmother from whom I have quoted before. She said, "These years are so wonderful that I can hardly believe they are mine."

But they are undeniably our own, our grandmother years. Enjoy!

Index